World War II
Aerial Combat
1937–1945

World War II Aerial Combat 1937–1945

The Allied and Axis Air Forces
A Visual History

Donald Nijboer

Firefly Books

Published by Firefly Books Ltd. 2025

First printing

Library of Congress Control Number: 2025936119

Library and Archives Canada Cataloguing in Publication
Title: World War II aerial combat, 1937-1945 : the Allied and Axis air forces : a visual history / Donald Nijboer.
Names: Nijboer, Donald, 1959- author
Description: First edition. | Includes index.
Identifiers: Canadiana 20250188740 | ISBN 9780228105879 (hardcover)
Subjects: LCSH: World War, 1939-1945—Aerial operations—Pictorial works. | LCSH: Air forces—History—20th century—Pictorial works. | LCSH: Airplanes, Military—Pictorial works. | LCGFT: Illustrated works.
Classification: LCC D785 .N55 2025 | DDC 940.54/40222—dc23

Published in the United States by
Firefly Books (U.S.) Inc.
P.O. Box 1338, Ellicott Station
Buffalo, New York 14205

Published in Canada by
Firefly Books Ltd.
50 Staples Avenue, Unit 1
Richmond Hill, Ontario L4B 0A7

Cover design: Hartley Millson
Interior design: Stacey Cho

Cover photos copyright: Author's Collection

Printed in China | E

We gratefully acknowledge the financial support of the Government of Canada for our publishing program.

CONTENTS

Introduction

Soldiers and sailors in many nations are apt to forget what they owe to the air forces.
– Field Marshal Montgomery after the victory at Alamein, November 1942.

World War I saw the rapid evolution and unprecedented development of the combat aircraft. Just 12 short years after the Wright brothers' first flight, aircraft had morphed from simple reconnaissance and artillery spotting platforms into fighter aircraft and bombers and there were even initial experiments with carrier borne aircraft.

The emergence of military aircraft added a new dimension to warfare and changed the battlefield forever. While combat aircraft in World War I had shown great promise, their effect on the battlefield was marginal since the technology, tactics and the application of air power on the ground were still in their infancy. After the war, however, airpower advocates began to see the potential of these new aircraft as a means of delivering troops behind enemy lines, destroying an opponent's transportation links as well as making direct attacks on enemy ground troops and naval forces on the high seas.

These objectives led to the formation of the world's first air forces independent of traditional land and naval forces. The Finnish Air Force was formed on 6 March 1918, followed by the Royal Air Force (RAF) on 1 April 1918. But many nation's air forces remained under the control of the army. The U.S. Army Air Services, later to become the U.S. Army Air Corps, was formed in 1926, just after the Imperial Japanese Army Air Force was established in 1925.

Between the two world wars, air power advocates, including Brig. Gen. William "Billy" Mitchell of the U.S. Army Air Services, Gen. Guilo Douhet of the Italian Air Force and Air Marshal Sir Hugh Trenchard, first commander of the RAF, regarded strategic bombing as a preferred alternative to the land battles of attrition that had cost so many lives in World War I. Bombers could simply fly over land-based armies, fortifications and high seas fleets.

They also believed that bombing could win wars outright by destroying the morale of the enemy's civilian populations at the same time as the bombs destroyed their industrial capacity to produce arms and munitions.

At the time these theories were being developed, the aircraft available for use were still left over from World War I. Most of the aircraft available in the late 1920s were too small and fragile to be of any real use and lacked bomb-carrying capability. When U.S. Army Air Corps aircraft sank the captured German battleship *Ostfrieland* in 1921, it was seen as a clear example of the ascendance of the bomber over the battleship. But this was a rigged demonstration. The *Ostfrieland* was a stationary target, bombed at low-level and had no anti-aircraft defenses. Had the ship been allowed to maneuver at sea, the chances of it being hit would have been minimal at best.

By the mid-1930s, aircraft design and materials had improved significantly. The introduction of the Martin B-10 monoplane in 1933 represented a huge leap forward in aeronautical technology and engineering. Using an all-metal construction, the B-10 was equipped with retractable landing gear, a rotating front turret,

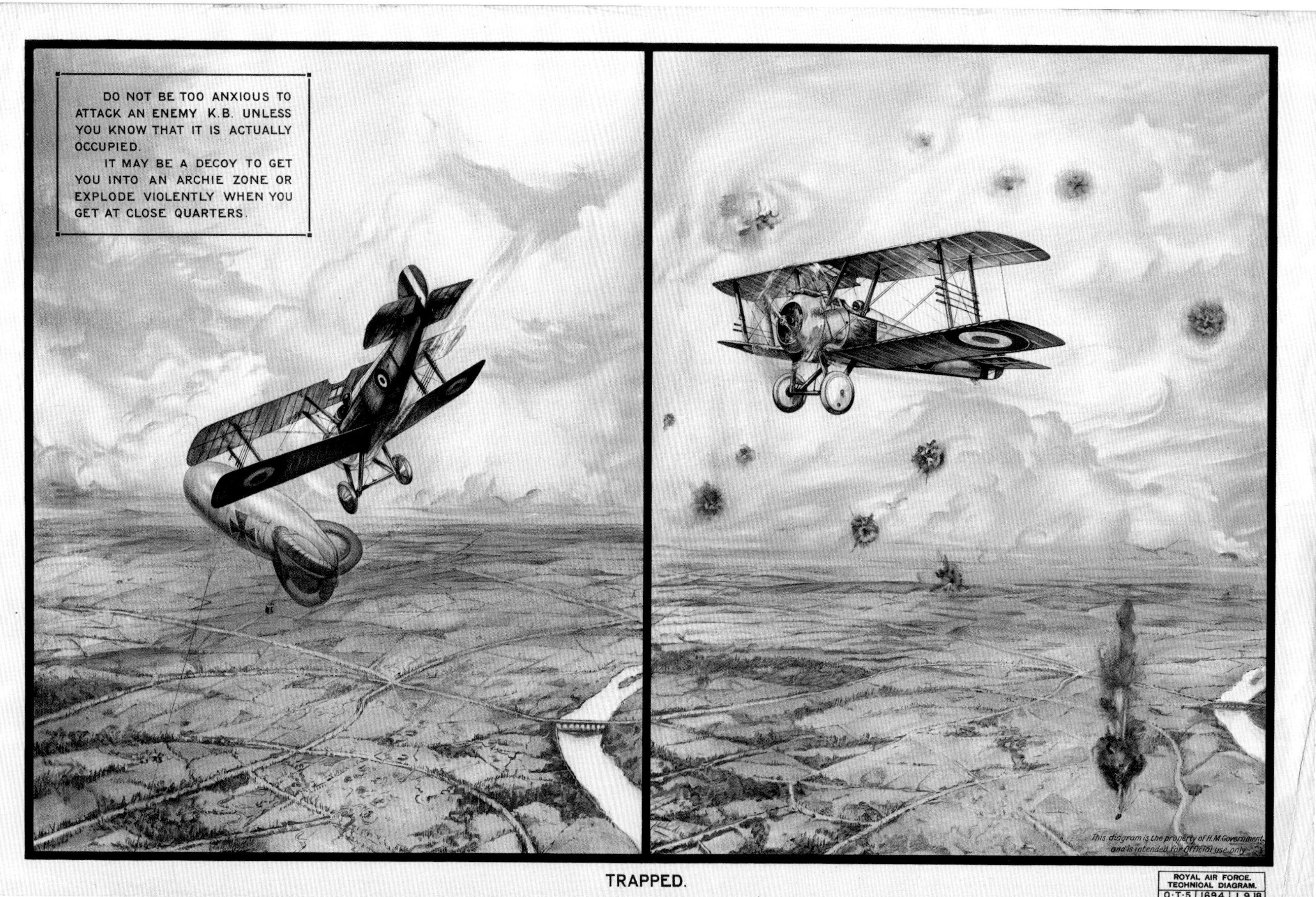

Air combat methods and tactics developed quickly during World War I, mostly by trial and error. This training poster highlights the dangers of attacking a German observation balloon unless you can see that it contains an observer. (CWM)

Two Martin B-10 bombers at March Field, California, in November 1935. 128 B-10A/B's entered service with the U.S. Army Air Force in 1934. By 1941 a handful still remained assigned to the defense of the Philippines. (NARA)

A Curtiss P-36C Hawk of 27th Pursuit Squadron in 1939, one of 1,095 P-36's that were produced. Most of the Hawks' combat missions were flown by French, Dutch, British, South African and Finnish pilots. (NARA)

an internal bomb bay, full engine cowlings, flaps, variable pitch propellers and a fully enclosed glass cockpit. Capable of reaching 213 mph in level flight, the new B-10 made all previous biplane bombers and existing fabric-covered fighters obsolete. The B-10 set the design template for all the bombers that followed and was still in service at the beginning of World War II. It saw action with the Royal Netherlands East Indies Army in 1941, the Chinese Air Force in 1937 and a handful were on charge with the U.S. Army Air Corps in the Philippines at the time of the Japanese attack on 7 December 1941.

Fighter design soon caught up to bomber design, and the fabric-covered biplane was replaced by the all-metal monoplane fighter. At the end of May 1935, both the first Messerschmitt Bf 109 and the American Curtiss P-36 fighters had taken flight. The Supermarine Spitfire would be in the air in March 1936.

In 1935 Adolf Hitler formerly announced the existence of the new Luftwaffe. Although many had seen it coming, the announcement sent shock waves throughout Europe. Now, one of the most important factors for any country's defense was the ability to produce well-equipped modern aircraft ready for combat. Air forces across the continent scrambled to rearm with the acquisition of new aircraft being the priority. For nations that had small aircraft industries, or none at all, the only way to bolster the size of their air force was to acquire aircraft from abroad. For the major powers, Britain, the United States, Germany, France, Japan, the Soviet Union and Italy, rearmament was easier due to their well-established aircraft industries with a sufficient workforce to produce combat aircraft at an accelerated rate.

The coming war would see the full potential of air power to dominate the battlefields and oceans. From mere appendages of the army and navy, air forces became essential tools of destruction and were crucial for success in battlefield and naval operations. New strategies and tactics were developed and tested. In World War II, some air forces succumbed to crushing defeats while others, bruised and battered, punched above their

The Supermarine Spitfire Mk V was the most widely produced British fighter of World War II. The Spitfire was flown by more foreign pilots than any other fighter, and it saw service both on land and as a carrier-based fighter, where it was known as the Seafire. (NASM)

weight. Many, after a slow start, learned quickly and wielded extraordinary power over the battlespace.

The history of air power and the air forces that fought in World War II can be divided into three categories: the victorious, the vanquished and the forgotten. Most of the histories and narratives of the war focus on the success of the German Luftwaffe during the "Blitzkrieg years," the rise and success of the Royal Air Force and Commonwealth Air Forces, the U.S. Army Air Forces, U.S. Navy Air Forces, the early exploits of the Japanese Naval and Army Air Forces and, to a lesser extent, the Soviet Air Forces.

The forgotten air forces on the Allied side include the Polish, Dutch, French, Belgian, Norwegian, Greek, Chinese and Yugoslavian air forces. All of these fought with determination and some with great skill against overwhelming odds. In just five days of fighting against German forces in May 1940, the tiny Dutch Air Force and anti-aircraft defenses inflicted significant losses on the enemy with 454 Luftwaffe aircraft destroyed or forced down over Dutch territory. The total German aircraft destroyed include: 47 Bf 109's, 14 Bf 110's, 40 He 111's, seven Ju 87's, 28 Ju 88's, nine Do 17's, four Do 215's, six He 59's, three He 115's, two Hs 123's, 10 Hs 126's and 284 Ju 52/3m's.

A Luftwaffe Bf 109E-1 on De Kooy Airfield, Netherlands, after being shot down by 2e Luitenant H. J. van Overvest in a Fokker D.XXI during the German invasion of the Netherlands in May 1940. (NIMH)

When one compares this with the 42 Luftwaffe bombers and 36 fighters shot down by the Royal Air Force during the 10 days of the evacuation of British and French troops from Dunkirk during the last week of May 1940, the accomplishment of the Dutch Air Force is even more remarkable.

The Axis Air Forces that fought alongside Germany have also been largely overlooked and forgotten, with little or no mention in most histories of the war. In the 1946–1947 edition of the respected encyclopedia *Jane's Fighting Aircraft of World War II*, for example, there is no mention of the Bulgarian, Romanian, Hungarian, Croatian, Vichy-France or Slovakian air forces. The Italian Air Force is rarely mentioned even though it fought on several fronts including in Russia, the Mediterranean, Italy, North Africa, Yugoslavia, Albania, Greece, Belgium, France and Ethiopia/Eritrea. The exploits of the tiny Finnish Air Force against the numerically superior Soviet forces during the Winter War in 1939–1940 and the Continuation War in 1941–1944 has also been largely ignored.

In 1941 the Romanian, Hungarian, Finnish, Italian, Slovakian and Croatian air forces contributed nearly 980 aircraft to Operation *Barbarossa*, the German invasion of the Soviet Union. The Luftwaffe committed 2,598 frontline aircraft. Like Hitler,

This photo reveals that Fiat used very inefficient production methods. Four different types of aircraft are being built at the same time — the Fiat CR.42 fighter, the BR.20 bomber, the CR.25 fighter and the G.12 transport aircraft. (Author's Collection)

each nation believed it would be a short war, and the spoils would go to the victors so were eager to participate.

While the number of aircraft from these countries might have seemed impressive, Hitler's interest in their participation was initially limited and viewed with some scepticism. That would change during the war. As German losses mounted, the Luftwaffe increasingly relied on the smaller air forces of its Eastern Allies. Germany was initially reluctant to supply new combat aircraft to its allies, often sending obsolete or well-used aircraft. But as losses mounted, newer types like the Bf 109E/F/G fighter, Junkers Ju 88, Ju 87, Heinkel He 111 and Dornier Do 17 bombers were delivered, giving these small air forces better operational punch. In many cases, as the war situation worsened, Hitler's allies had to fight on their own with little support from the Germans. And when Allied heavy and medium bombers began to attack targets in Germany beginning in 1943, the Luftwaffe was forced to allocate its air power resources between the Russian front, the Italian front and those fighter squadrons reserved for homeland air defense.

The shifting tides of war and military circumstances also caused some other air forces to be split in two. The Free French Air Force and the Vichy-French air forces fought alongside the Allies and Axis at the same time. The Italian Air Force would fracture in 1943, with the Republican Air Force (*Aeronautica Rebbulicana Nationale – ANR*) fighting with the Germans and the Regia Aeronautica (*Aeronautica Co-Belligerent*) joining the Allies.

In the Pacific and the China/Burma/India (CBI) theaters of war, the Japanese fought alone. As the war progressed, Japan found itself battling the combined air forces of the U.S. Navy/Marine Corps, U.S. Army Air Force, the Royal Australian Air Force, the Royal New Zealand Air Force, the Royal Air Force, the Royal Canadian Air Force, the Royal Navy Fleet Air Arm, the Royal Indian Air Force, the Chinese Air Force and, in the last few days of the war, the Soviet Air Forces.

On the eve of war in Europe and contrary to many histories, the vaunted German Luftwaffe was far from prepared to go to war in 1939. With just months to plan for the invasion of Poland — code named *Fall Weiss* — many squadrons were still equipped with obsolete aircraft, there was an alarming shortage of bombs, and the training of many aircrews was far from complete. Luftwaffe intelligence about its adversaries was another huge liability that would plague it throughout the war. But even with the Luftwaffe's deficiencies, it was far superior to the Polish Air Force. At dawn on 1 September 1939, the Luftwaffe committed 810 medium bombers, 340 Ju 87 Stukas and 240 fighters to the invasion. To meet the onslaught the Poles mustered 460 first-line combat aircraft. On 3 September, in support of Poland, Britain and France declared war on Germany.

A Bf 109E of 3.(J)/LG 2 preparing for a mission over Poland in September 1939. Sixty-seven Bf 109's were lost during the invasion. It was a high number considering the relatively limited number of Bf 109 *Jagdbruppen*'s committed to the campaign. (Author's Collection)

The Allied Air Forces

A Curtiss Hawk III Chinese aircraft that was shot down circa 1937. By February 1938 the Chinese had practically no combat-worthy Hawk III's remaining. With the arrival of Soviet aircraft, the remaining Hawks were relegated to second-line duties. (USNHHC)

CHINA

Chinese Air Force

China is the first nation to be profiled here because it was the first of what would become the Allied air forces to engage in combat with what would become the Axis powers. As Europe began to slowly rearm in earnest, China was already receiving aircraft from abroad. In July 1937 full-scale war between China and Japan began. This pitted the Chinese Air Force, which had 600 aircraft of which only 230 were operational, against the Japanese Army Air force and the Japanese Naval Air Force. Initially, the Chinese Air Force relied on American, German, Italian and British aircraft: the American Curtiss Hawk II fighter, Martin B-10 bomber, British Gloster Gladiator, Italian Fiat CR.32 fighter and early versions of the German Heinkel He 111 bomber.

One of biggest exporters of aircraft to China was the Soviet Union, which supplied 1,250 fighters and bombers between 1937 and 1939. Of that total, 216 were Polikarpov I-16's, 347 were 1-15's and 100 were 1-153 fighters. By 1940 relations between the Soviet Union and Chiang Kai-shek's government began to cool, and soon all military aid was canceled and Soviet volunteers withdrawn from China. The introduction of the Mitsubishi A5M2 "Claude," Nakajima Ki-27 "Nate" and the vaunted A6M2 "Zero" fighters all but guaranteed the Japanese air supremacy over China in 1940. In response, the Chinese acquired the 180 Republic P-43 Lancers and ordered 129 Vultee P-66 Vanguards in 1940.

The Japanese invasion of French Indochina in March 1941 lead directly to a Lend Lease agreement with the United States. This was quickly followed by an order by China for 1,000 aircraft to assist in the fight against Japan.

Combat Aircraft Available August 1937

Fighters: 305

Light bombers/reconnaissance: 295

CHINA

The Curtiss A-12 was a two-seat attack aircraft first ordered by the U.S. Army Air Corps. It entered service in 1932. In 1936 the Chinese Aviation Commission placed an order for 20 A-12's. These aircraft equipped the 26th and 27th Squadrons of the Chinese's 9th Bomber Group. (NARA)

When America declared war against Japan in 1941, China became a very important ally. In this poster the heroic imagery of China fighting alone implores the viewer to donate to the United China Relief Fund. U.S. Army Air Force units and personnel did not arrive in China until July 1942 with the formation of the China Air Task Force (CATF). It was a tiny force, three fighter squadrons equipped with Curtiss P-40's and one with North American B-25 Mitchell bombers. (LOC)

The Curtiss Hawk III's performance was comparable to the Fiat CR.32, the Gloster Gauntlet and the Grumman F3F-1. It could double as a light bomber and with an external drop tank had good range. At the beginning of the Sino-Japanese War in July 1937 the Hawk III was the primary fighter of the Chinese Air Force. (Author's Collection)

Soviet Polikarpov I-153's were supplied to the Chinese Central Government early in 1940. These fighters remained in first-line service well into 1943. They had a top speed of 264 mph at 16,400 feet. This aircraft was flown by Chinese ace Liu Chi Sheng, who was credited with ten individual and two shared aerial victories against the Japanese. (Author's Collection)

This Curtiss Hawk 81A of the 23rd Fighter Group American Volunteer Group (AVG) is flying over Burma in 1942. The arrival of the American Volunteer Group, made up of 100 Hawk 81A fighters along with pilots and ground crew, was a huge boost to the Chinese Air Force. From 18 December 1941 until 4 July 1942, the pilots of the American Volunteer Group dominated the skies over free China, northern Burma and the Assam Valley in India. (NARA)

A Chinese Air Force Republic P-43A Lancer. In 1942, 180 Lancers were shipped to China. The P-43A-1 had a top speed of 355 mph at 20,000 feet and was armed with two .50-caliber and two .30-caliber machine guns. It was used by the Chinese Air Force against the Japanese until December 1943. (NARA)

A brand-new PZL 37 Los stands ready for inspection. Its sleek design and impressive performance made it one of the most advanced bombers in the world at the beginning of World War II. (Author's Collection)

POLAND

Polish Air Force

Poland, like many other European countries, had its own domestic military aircraft industry and was able to produce aircraft for itself and for export. It also manufactured many foreign aircraft designs under license. The major aircraft manufacturer was Panstwowe Zaklady Lotnicze (PZL). Even though Poland could manufacture its own fighters and bombers, it did try to buy aircraft from France and the United States, but to no avail. An order for 143 Hawk H-75A's worth $8 million was canceled on 21 July 1939 due to Poland's lack of hard currency. Britain did supply nine Hawker Hurricanes, but they did not reach Poland before the country was overrun in September 1939.

One of the best medium bombers in the world prior to the outbreak of war was the twin-engine PZL 37 Los. Top speed was 295mph and in 1937, 36 were ordered for the Polish air force. With its high top speed and a bombload capacity of 5,690 pounds, the company soon had export orders from Yugoslavia, Bulgaria, Romania, Turkey and Greece. Poland also exported its gull-winged fighter the PZL P.11 and PZL P.24 to Romania, Bulgaria and Greece. At the outbreak of war Poland stood ready with 158 PZL 11c's, 30 PZL 7a fighters and 36 PZL 37 Los and 50 PZL 23 light bombers.

A PZL P.11c of No. 161 (Turkeys) Squadron. The P.11 would have the honor of recording the Allies' first air-to-air victory of the war. On 1 September 1939, Wladyslaw Gnys shot down a Dornier Do 17P over Krakow, one of four Do 17's shot down that day. (Author's Collection)

Combat Aircraft Available September 1939
Fighters: 188
Bombers: 86

POLAND

The all-metal PZL 23 "Karaś" (Crucian Carp) light bomber first flew in 1935. At the outbreak of war 117 were available for combat. Armament consisted of three 7.92 mm machine guns, and it was capable of carrying a bombload of 1,540 pounds. After the fall of Poland, 21 PZL 23 bombers were shipped to Romania. Nineteen of them were kept by the Romanians and were used against the Soviet Union after the launch of Operation *Barbarossa* in June 1941. (Author's Collection)

The PZL 37 Los (Moose) bomber was powered by two Bristol Pegasus XX radial engines rated at 940 horsepower each. Armament consisted of three 7.92 mm machine guns, and the aircraft could carry 5,690 pounds of bombs. (Author's Collection)

A PZL 37 Los being made ready for flight. In 1938, it was considered the world's finest medium bomber. As fast as the contemporary Blenheim, Tupolev SB-2 and Do 17, the Los could carry more than double the bombload much further than the other aircraft in a surprisingly compact and sleek airframe. (Author's Collection)

A PZL P.11c of No. 114 (Fighting Cocks) Squadron in the summer of 1939. The P.11c was a gull wing, all-metal fighter with a conventional layout, fixed landing gear and an open cockpit. Powered by a 565-horsepower engine, it had a top speed of 242 mph. Armament consisted of four 7.7 mm machine guns. (Author's Collection)

A row of Curtiss-Tomahawk IIB's of No. 3 Royal Australian Air Force Squadron line up at Lydda, Palestine. In May 1940 No. 3 Squadron received its first Tomahawks and immediately began preparations to get them combat ready for the forthcoming invasion of Vichy French Syria, code named Operation *Exporter*. (Author's Collection)

GREAT BRITAIN and the COMMONWEALTH NATIONS

Royal Air Force

As the threat of Germany's rearmament became real, the British response was to ramp up aircraft production and develop a series of "Schemes" between 1934 and 1939. Five Schemes were passed by the cabinet: A, C, F, L and M. The first Scheme, adopted in July 1934, called for a frontline strength of 1,544 aircraft of which 1,252 were for home defense. When the size of Luftwaffe became known in 1935, Scheme C replaced Scheme A and called for the addition of 1,500 aircraft. In April 1938 the Cabinet approved Scheme L, which envisioned a frontline strength of 2,373 aircraft, a significant increase from the 1,735 level of Scheme F.

Aircraft production increased more than threefold from fewer than 200 aircraft a month in each of the first six months of 1938 to 630 per month in the first six months of 1939. In 1938, to bolster its numbers, Britain, like other nations, turned to America with an order for 200 Lockheed Hudson light bombers. At the outbreak of war, the Royal Air Force had 773 fighters and 1,313 bombers on strength. Of that total, just 306 were Supermarine Spitfires, their best fighter. The rest was made up of Hawker Hurricanes, Bolton Paul Defiant and Gloster Gladiators. Bomber Command had a mixed force of Handley Page Hampden, Armstrong Whitley, Vickers Wellington, Bristol Blenheim medium bombers and the obsolete single engine Fairey Battle. Coastal Command had 19 Squadrons with a mix of Short Sunderland, Avro Anson, Lockheed Hudson, Vickers Vildebeest, Saro London and Supermarine Stranners. The Navy's Fleet Air Arm had 232 aircraft, most of which were the fabric-covered Fairey Swordfish torpedo bombers.

Shortly after the outbreak of war, the Royal Air Force was quickly augmented by the Royal Canadian Air Force (RCAF), Royal New Zealand Air Force (RNZAF), Royal Australian Air Force (RAAF) and the South African Air Force (SAAF).

The Royal Air Force also benefited from tens of thousands of Commonwealth volunteers along with thousands of foreign nationals (Polish, Czech, French, Dutch, Norwegian, Belgian and Greek) from the occupied countries who volunteered to continue the fight starting in 1940. In essence the Royal Air Force became a multi-national air force. There were also thousands of Americans who volunteered and joined the RCAF and RAF. While the Canadian, New Zealand, Australian, South African and Indian air forces were separate entitles, their individual squadrons mostly served under RAF command. In the Pacific, New Zealand, Australian and Canadian units also served under a unified Allied Command and did not act independently.

Combat Aircraft Available September 1939

Fighters: 773

Bombers: 1,313

COASTAL COMMAND

Maritime Patrol Aircraft: 242

Fleet Air Arm: 232

A Northrop Delta and Hawker Hurricane Mk I running up its engine, Vancouver 1939. The Delta served the Royal Canadian Air Force as a high-performance photo reconnaissance aircraft and was the first all-metal stressed-skinned aircraft built under license in Canada. The RCAF received its first Hurricanes in February 1939. This example does not have its armament fitted. During the war a total of 1,451 Hurricanes were built by the Canadian Car and Foundry Company. (CVA)

Royal Canadian Air Force (RCAF)

Shortly after the end of World War I, the Canadian Air Force (CAF) was established in 1920. Four years later, the CAF was granted the royal title becoming the Royal Canadian Air Force. Protected by three oceans and no hostile nations on its borders, the Royal Canadian Air Force remained static in size and equipment with most of its work in the 1920s and 1930s being civilian in nature, with forest and coastal patrols and artic surveying among their duties.

At the outbreak of war, the Canadians like the Australian, New Zealand, and South African air forces were caught unprepared. But that was understandable given the fact they had no hostile nations threatening their borders or cities from direct air attack.

The RCAF had just 20 squadrons, eight regular and 12 auxiliaries, most of which were understrength except for No. 1 Squadron RCAF, which was equipped with Hawker Hurricanes and was somewhat ready for combat. On the eve of war, the Canadian manpower was 4,061 officers and airmen. Aircraft strength was a mixed bag of 270 aircraft of 28 different types which included: 22 Westland Wapitis, 20 Airspeed Oxfords, 19 Hawker Hurricanes, 13 Armstrong Whitworth Atlas's, 12 Canadian Vickers Deltas, 11 Blackburn Sharks, 10 Fairey Battles, nine Canadian Vickers Stranraers, five Armstrong Whitworth Siskins, four Noorduyn Norsemen and four Vickers Vancouvers.

Canada's contribution to the Allied air war effort was immense. One of the first and most important contributions Canada made was the British Commonwealth Air Training Plan. Under a deal singed in 1939, Canada agreed to provide air bases and facilities to provide training for airmen and ground crews from every part of the Commonwealth. At its peak the Air Training Plan consisted of 3,540 aircraft and 33,000 air force personnel.

An Armstrong Whitworth Siskin Mk III of No. 21 Training Squadron RCAF, Camp Borden Ontario. The Siskin, a single-seat biplane fighter from the 1920s, was one of the first new fighters to enter Royal Air Force and Royal Canadian Air Force service after World War I. Between 1926 and 1939, the RCAF operated a sizable fleet of Siskins. (Author's Collection)

By the end of the war the Royal Canadian Air Force grew to become the fourth largest air force in the world with 47 squadrons serving overseas and 28 squadrons assigned to continental defense.

Two Commonwealth Aircraft Corporation CA-13 Boomerangs prepare for takeoff in Bougainville in the Solomon Islands chain. Built in response to Australia's urgent need for fighter aircraft at the beginning of the war, the Boomerang utilized the design principles and construction techniques of the Wirraway advanced trainer, already in production. Boomerangs were flown by No. 4, 5, 83, 84 and 85 Squadrons Royal Australian Air Force in a home defense role, undertaking escort duties for shipping convoys and ground attack operations against the Japanese. (RNZAFM)

Royal Australian Air Force (RAAF)

On 21 March 1921 the formation of the Australian Air Force as an independent force was officially announced. Later that year on 13 August, the new force became the Royal Australian Air Force. In 1927 their only combat aircraft were a handful of World War I de Havilland DH.9 bombers. In February 1934 Australia ordered its first modern aircraft with the purchase of 18 Hawker Demon two-seater fighters from Great Britain. Sixty-four more would follow, equipping seven squadrons.

In late 1938, as part of an earlier British order, the Australian government placed an order for 50 American Lockheed Hudson light bombers to replace its aging Avro Ansons. These were the first American combat aircraft ordered by Australia and more would follow. By December 1941 the RAAF had received 152 Hudsons. Developed from the civilian Lockheed Model 14 Super Electra, the Hudson was a huge improvement over the slower and less capable Anson. With a top speed of 252 mph it could carry 1,600 pounds of bombs.

Like the other Commonwealth air forces, the Royal Australian Air Force was ill-prepared for war, but the Australian government quickly offered to send six squadrons to Britain to join the fight against Germany. This idea was, however, quickly shelved when it was realized that a force of that size, the entire RAAF at the time, was impossible to implement. At the outbreak of war, the RAAF had just 310 officers and 3,179 airmen. At the time, more Australian pilots (400) were serving in the Royal Air Force in the United Kingdom than with the Royal Australian Air Force at home.

When war in Europe broke out, the Australians had 246 aircraft on strength which included: 82 Avro Ansons, 54 Hawker Demons, 7 CAC Wirraways, 21 Supermarine Walrus's and a mixed bag of 82 training aircraft.

Between 1934 and 1936 the RAAF purchased 64 Hawker Demon two seat biplane fighters from Great Britain. Powered by the 600-horsepower Rolls-Royce Kestrel engine, the Demon had a top speed of 182 mph and was armed with two forward-firing Vickers .303-caliber machine guns and a rear-firing Lewis gun. By 1939 these aircraft were mostly used in the army cooperation role and for training purposes. (Author's Collection)

In 1937, 29 ex-RAF Blackburn Baffin torpedo bombers were acquired by the RNZAF. The Baffin could lift a 2,000-pound bombload or one 1,576-pound torpedo. These aircraft equipped the newly formed Territorial Squadrons based at Wellington, Christchurch and Auckland, all of which were operational by September 1939. (Author's Collection)

Royal New Zealand Air Force (RNZAF)

In 1923 New Zealand established the New Zealand Permanent Air Force, which had just 11 full-time staff. They were backed up by the New Zealand Air Force (NZAF), which was an all-volunteer territorial unit made up of 100 personnel. In 1937 the government passed the Air Force Act, which established the newly named Royal New Zealand Air Force as an independent arm of the military. Despite expansion efforts, New Zealand Air Force was unprepared for the outbreak of war in September 1939. With just 756 full-time personnel, the air force had just 58 combat aircraft made up of 19 Vickers Vildebeests and 29 Blackburn Baffin B-5 torpedo bombers. Both were 1930s vintage fabric-covered biplane aircraft.

Approximately 420 New Zealanders were serving in the Royal Air Force at the outbreak of war in Europe, the most from any of the commonwealth nations. At the time, the Royal New Zealand Air Force was considered as a purely training organization that supplied pilots and aircrew to the Royal Air Force. During the first 12 months of the war, they transitioned from a training organization into a combat force by arming all available aircraft with machine guns and bomb racks. By December 1941 the Royal New Zealand Air Force had expanded to include 641 aircraft, the majority being used as trainers. Combat aircraft included 36 newly acquired Lockheed Hudsons, 48 Vickers Vincents, 26 Vildebeests and two Short Singapore III flying boats. Personnel had grown to 17,000, with 10,500 in New Zealand, 1,100 in Canada and some 3,600 serving in the Royal Air Force.

Aerial view of No. 486 Squadron Royal New Zealand Air Force Tempest V NV763 SA-Z. Fighters like the high-performance Tempest Mk V and Spitfire Mk XIV were held back from use on D-Day and the Battle of Normandy to counter the V-1 Flying Bomb attacks on London. No. 486 was the second highest scoring squadron with 246 V-1's shot down. (RNZAFM)

GREAT BRITAIN and the COMMONWEALTH NATIONS

At the outbreak of war, Royal Air Force Fighter Command had four Auxiliary Squadrons overseas that were equipped with the Gloster Gladiator II. In Egypt, No. 33 and 80 Squadrons were joined by the newly formed No. 112 Squadron. In Aden, No. 94 Squadron was formed to defend the port. (RNZAFM)

This Royal New Zealand Air Force Vickers Vildebeest torpedo bomber is equipped with a long-range fuel tank and two 250-pound bombs. In 1941 the New Zealand Air Force had 39 Vildebeests on strength. The Royal Air Force had two more Vildebeest-equipped squadrons based in Singapore at the time of the Japanese invasion in 1942. (RNZAFM)

This photograph of a factory-fresh Spitfire Mk Ia P9450 in flight in April 1940 shows the black and white wing half-tone underside camouflage pattern. The black and white underside was used to aid in the identification of friendly aircraft. By June 1940 this camouflage pattern was replaced by a sky-blue underside. This change was made after Royal Air Force fighter pilots found it hard to spot German Bf 109's, whose undersides were lightly painted and blended with the blue sky above the aircraft. (Author's Collection)

This photo shows the expansive wing of the Armstrong Whitworth Whitely Mk V bomber. This one was attached to No. 78 Squadron and has 36 mission markings on its nose. The Mk V could carry 7,000 pounds of bombs, which was significantly more than the Royal Air Force's other medium bombers. (RNZAFM)

Two torpedo-armed Hampdens in formation flying low over the North Sea. These aircraft are believed to be from No. 489 Squadron Royal New Zealand Air Force. In total, 1,432 Hampdens were built, which included 160 that were manufactured in Canada. (RNZAFM)

On the ground, the Short Stirling was an imposing aircraft. This No. 218 Squadron Stirling participated in Operation *Glimmer* on D-Day, dropping "window," metallic strips of foil that were used to confuse enemy radar and deceive the Germans as to the actual landing beaches being used by the Allies. (Author's Collection)

A No. 257 Squadron Hawker Typhoon Mk IB in August 1943. The Typhoon had the reputation of being a technical nightmare. The problem of carbon monoxide leaking into the cockpit was never fully solved and the Napier Sabre engine was extremely complicated, requiring constant maintenance. Originally designed to replace the Spitfire, it would go on to prove itself as an effective low-level ground-attack aircraft. The Typhoon was credited with 246 enemy air-to-air kills during the war. (Author's Collection)

Two Handley Page Halifax B II's from No. 35 Squadron undertake a training mission during the early summer of 1942. The Halifax was the second Royal Air Force's four-engine bomber to enter service. Unable to exceed altitudes of over 20,000 feet, the B II's suffered high combat attrition rates. By 1943 this forced Bomber Command to restrict the aircraft to the less hazardous targets. (Author's Collection)

The Halifax B II powered by four Merlin engines was never a graceful aircraft. Its bulbous nose turret, heavily framed bomb-aimer's position and large dorsal turret created excessive drag, degrading performance. A total of 1,977 B II's were built. (Author's Collection)

Shark-mouthed Spitfire Mk VIII's of No. 457 Squadron Royal Australian Air Force seen here at Morotai, Indonesia, in the summer of 1945. They flew in support of ground troops fighting the last remaining Japanese forces in New Guinea and Timor. (Author's Collection)

Completely obsolete at the beginning of the war, the Fairey Battle saw extensive service as a training aircraft. Here, two Battles based at Canadian Air Force Base, Trenton, warm up for another gunnery training flight. (Author's Collection)

An RAF Coastal Command Beaufighter Mk IC of No. 35 Squadron taxies out for another mission. This variant first entered service with No. 252 Squadron Coastal Command in Malta. The Beaufighter proved to be the RAF's most potent strike weapon of the war and served with the British, Canadian, Australian and New Zealand air forces in Europe, the Mediterranean, Burma, India and the Pacific. (Author's Collection)

This ground crew is pushing a bomb trolley with two Mk I aerial anti-shipping sea mines to be loaded into the bomb bay of a No. 75 Squadron Royal New Zealand Air Force Stirling. These mines were laid in the waters outside of German harbors and in known merchant shipping routes around occupied Europe. During the war, Royal Air Force Bomber Command laid 47,307 mines. (RNZAFM)

Aerial view of a No. 179 Squadron Wellington HX379 WN-A in October 1942. This aircraft is fitted with ASV Mark II anti-submarine radar, as shown by the "stickleback" aerial array on top of the fuselage. (RNZAFM)

On 25 September 1942, Royal Air Force Coastal Command Beaufighters attacked shipping off the coast of Den Helder, Holland. Eight air-to-surface anti-shipping rockets can be seen on the left and right streaking toward their intended target. Five other Beaufighters can be seen in this photo. (RNZAFM)

A Short Sunderland flying boat in flight over the water. The Sunderland served as one of the most powerful and widely used Allied flying boats throughout the war. In addition to the Royal Air Force, the aircraft was used by the Canadian, Australian, New Zealand and South African air forces. At the outbreak of war, RAF Coastal Command had just 40 Sunderlands on strength. (RNZAFM)

This Coastal Command Boeing Fortress GR Mk IIA is being loaded with depth charges. ASV Mk II radar antennas, one of the most effective for U-Boat hunting, are visible on the nose and beneath the port wing. (Author's Collection)

A Vickers Wellington Mk III from No. 419 Squadron Royal Canadian Air Force. Powered by two Bristol Hercules 14-cylinder twin-row radial engines with 1,500 horsepower each, the Wellington had a top speed of 216 mph at 12,500 feet. No. 419 later converted to the Halifax and then to Lancasters. Over a span of three and half years, No. 419 Squadron logged 400 operational missions and dropped 14,000 tons of bombs and mines. (Author's Collection)

Pilot Officer Len Farr instructing a Malayan ground crew as they push back a No. 488 Squadron Royal New Zealand Air Force Brewster Buffalo I in Singapore in 1941. Not considered fit for combat in Europe, the British assigned the Buffalo to the defense of Singapore and Malaya. A number of squadrons were established and primarily manned by Australian and New Zealand pilots. (RNZAFM)

P-47 Thunderbolts of No. 30 Squadron Royal Air Force taxi to their takeoff point past a line of Hawker Hurricane Mark IIC's, at Cox's Bazar, India. The P-47 first entered the war with the U.S. Army Air force in December 1942. In 1944 Royal Air Force South East Asia Command received their first P-47's to replace the venerable Hawker Hurricanes. (Author's Collection)

These Bristol Blenheim Mk IV's of No. 84 and 203 Squadrons are en route to attack Vichy French targets in Syria. More than 70 Squadrons, including units from Army Co-operation, Bomber, Coastal, Far East Bomber, Fighter and Middle East Commands, operated the Blenheim. (Author's Collection)

Officers and airmen, believed to be part of No. 5 Middle East Training School, Royal Air Force Station Shallufa, Egypt, inspect a line of aircraft consisting of a Bristol Beaufort, Beaufighter and Martin B-26 Marauder. (RNZAFM)

The Gloster Meteor was the first British jet fighter to enter operational service during World War II. Because of its excellent low-level speed performance, better than the Tempest V and Spitfire Mk XIV, it was assigned to battle the German V-1 flying bomb attacks during the summer of 1944. (Author's Collection)

A formation of RAAF Bristol Beauforts with bomb doors open begin their run onto their target at the Japanese base of Rabaul on New Britain Island. In October 1943, as resources increased, the Allies began a major offensive aimed at neutralizing Rabaul, which became the scene of almost incessant air attacks. Eventually, the isolated and much battered base was pounded into submission by almost 22,000 tons of bombs dropped by American, Australian and New Zealand aircraft. The neutralization of Rabaul took 12 months to accomplish and was a serious strategic defeat for the Japanese. (Author's Collection)

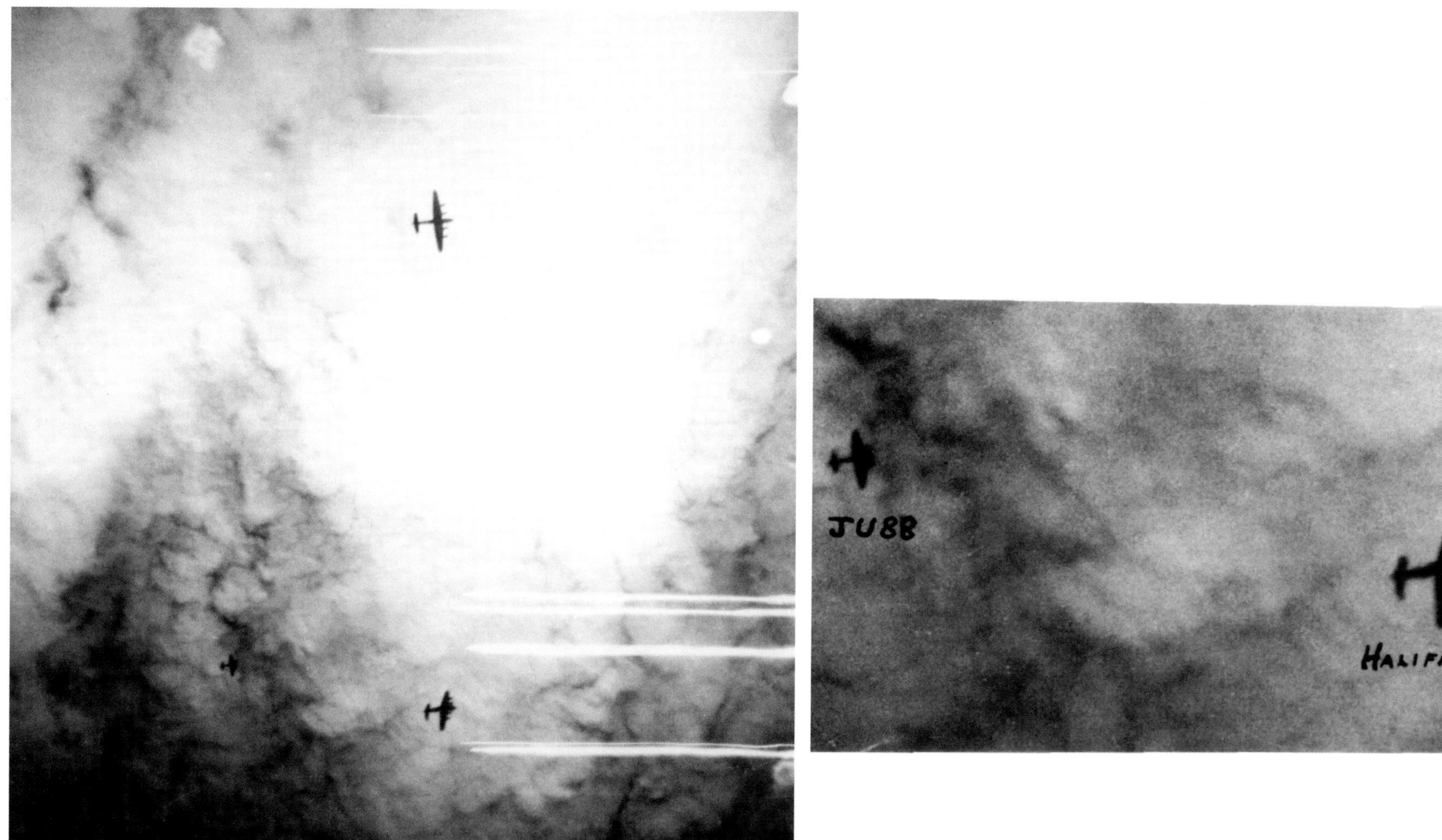

This is one of the only known photographs that shows a German Ju 88 night-fighter in pursuit of what appears to be a Lancaster bomber and not a Halifax as noted on the photo. This photo was taken during the last major raid of the war on Hamburg, 8–9 April 1945. (Author's Collection)

For Royal Air Force bomber crews to reach an important German target often meant flying through a pyrotechnic nightmare. During the attack run they would be met with a wall of searchlights, cascading target indicators, night fighter flares, tracers, flaming aircraft, smoke and fire from the ground and bursting flak. This photo shows the scene over Pfozrheim on the night of 23–24 February 1945. Twelve Lancasters were lost to flak, and the firestorm that was created by the bombing killed 17,600 people on the ground. (Author's Collection)

The 22,000-pound "Grand Slam" bomb seen here being loaded, could only be carried by specially modified Lancasters B1 Specials that were operated by No. 617 Squadron. A total of 41 "Grand Slams" were dropped before the war ended. (Author's Collection)

This Royal Air Force B-24 Liberator of No. 37 Squadron narrowly missed being hit by falling bombs dropped from another B-24. This photograph was taken during a raid on the shipyards at Monfalcone, Italy on 6 March 1945. (Author's Collection)

An aerial photograph of a No. 617 Squadron "Dambuster" Lancaster bomber on a training flight. The highly modified Lancaster was designated Type 464. It incorporated cut-away bomb doors, special calipers and a motor capable of spinning the top-secret four-ton bouncing bomb before it was dropped. (RNZAFM)

A 12,000-pound Tallboy bomb being loaded into a Lancaster Mk II. The first Tallboys were deployed on the night of 8 June 1944 by 25 modified Lancaster bombers. The attack caused extensive damage to the Saumur Railway Tunnel in France. By the end of the war, a total of 854 Tallboy bombs had been dropped. (RNZAFM)

A Fairey Swordfish of No. 824 NAS takes off from the escort carrier HMS *Striker*. The aircraft is armed with the advanced "Fido" homing torpedo. Once dropped, the torpedo would begin a circular search pattern. Once the propeller noise of a U-boat was detected, it would home in and strike its target. (Author's Collection)

A Hurricane-IIb of No. 1 Squadron the Royal Indian Air Force (RIAF) at Impha, India. The RIAF received 300 Hurricanes during the war that were operated in the China-Burma-India (CBI) theater until the last day of the war. (Author's Collection)

Fleet Air Arm (FAA) Martlet Mk II's Wildcats and Seafires ready for takeoff aboard HMS *Formidable* during Operation *Torch* in November 1942. For the operation, *Formidable* carried 24 Marlets and six Seafires. (Author's Collection)

Fairey Fulmars from No. 800 and 809 Naval Air Service wait to take off from HMS *Victorious*. The Fulmar was one of the forgotten British fighters of the war, but in service with the Fleet Air Arm it shot down more enemy aircraft than any other Fleet Air Arm fighter, with 112 aerial victories out of the 455 credited to all the fighters. (Mathew Willis)

Barracudas of No. 827 Naval Air Squadron prepare for takeoff aboard HMS *Victorious* during Operation *Tungsten*, the attack against the German battleship *Tirpitz*, on 3 April 1944. Barracuda pilots managed to hit the *Tirpitz* 12 times with a mix of 1,600-pound armor-piercing, 500-pound semi-armor-piercing and medium-capacity bombs. (Mathew Willis)

Seafire III's from No. 801 and 880 Naval Air Service run up their engines prior to launch on the deck of the HMS *Indefatigable*, part of the British Pacific Fleet, in early April 1945. To increase the Seafire's anemic range, they were equipped with either 90-gallon ex-P-40 drop tanks or slipper tanks. This gave the Seafire a range of just over 400 miles. The drop tanks were only dropped when they encountered enemy fighters. In the Pacific, Seafire pilots shot down 15 Zero-sen's. (Author's Collection)

A Firefly Mk I of No. 1770 Naval Air Service has its wings unfolded by deck crew in preparation for the Sumatra oil refinery raid on 25 January 1945. Unlike their American naval counterparts, most Fleet Air Arm aircraft did not have hydraulic wing-folding mechanisms. (Andrew Thomas)

HMS *Fledgling* was home to the Women's Flying Naval Service aircraft maintenance training courses. During the war, the FAA would use the greatest number of different carrier fighters, including the Skua, Roc, Sea Gladiator, Sea Hurricane, Fulmar, Seafire, Firefly, Marlet (Wildcat), Hellcat and Corsair. In comparison, the U.S. Navy used just three. This photo shows a Seafire, Corsair, two Wildcats, two Sea Hurricanes and a Fairey Fulmer. (Author's Collection)

The British Pacific Fleet is made ready for its participation in Operation *Iceberg*, the invasion of Okinawa, in March 1945. Designated as Task Force 57, its four fleet carriers were given the task of neutralizing Japanese airfields in the Sakishima Gunto archipelago. In this photograph FAA Avengers pound Hirara Airfield on Miyako island in early April 1945. (Frank Mitchell)

The Curtiss A-25 Shrike in Royal Australian Air Force colors. The A-25 was a modified version of the U.S. Navy's new SB2C Helldiver dive-bomber. The U.S. Army Air Corps ordered 100 A-25's in 1940. The Shrike was offered to Australia but only ten were accepted. After flight trials the poor performance and handling qualities of the aircraft became evident, and Australia rejected the remainder of the order. The U.S. Army Air Force sent the remaining 410 aircraft to the Marines. The A-25 never saw combat. (NASM)

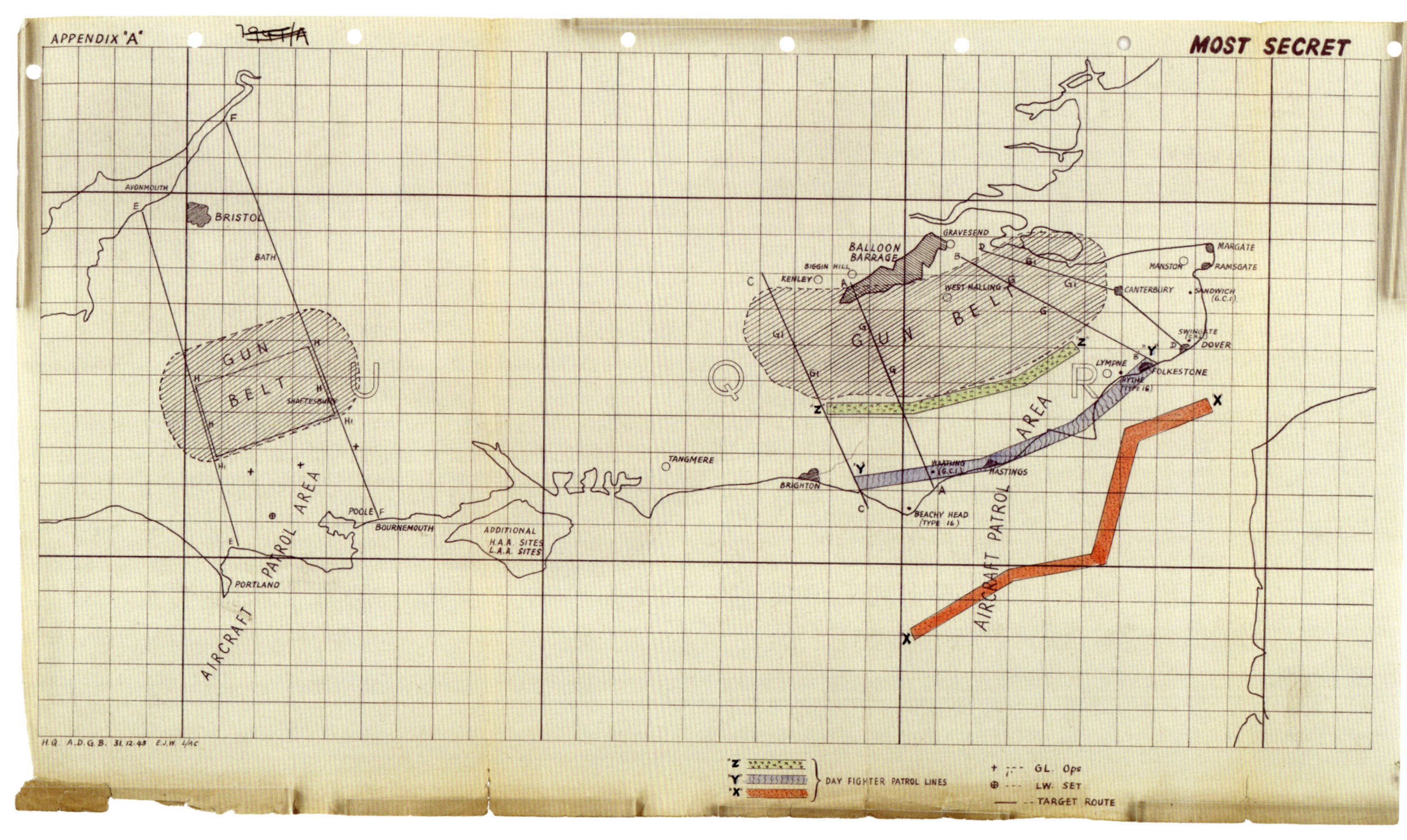

This "Most Secret" map shows the initial disposition of the defenses laid out to counter the German V-1 Flying Bombs aimed at London. Fighters flew standing patrols along three lines in blue, green and red. Behind the fighter patrol lines was the anti-aircraft gun zone followed by the balloon barrage zone. Royal Air Force fighters were responsible for the destruction of 2,250 V-1's during the war. (NARA)

The DeHavilland Mosquito, shown here in a cutaway drawing, is arguably the greatest combat aircraft of World War II. With an airframe made entirely from wood, the "wooden wonder" flew an incredible 39,795 sorties with the Royal Air Force Bomber Command. Only 260 were lost on operations for a loss rate of just 0.65 percent, the lowest of any aircraft in Bomber Command. (NARA)

These aircraft identification slides were used in Station Cinemas for training purposes. They depict the Spitfire, Mosquito and Mustang. During the war, aircraft recognition by anti-aircraft gunners and pilots on both sides was extremely poor. The result was far too many aircraft shot down by friendly fire. (RNZAFM)

MOSQUITO
SPAN 54 FT. LENGTH 40 FT.

MUSTANG
SPAN 37 FT. LENGTH 32 FT.

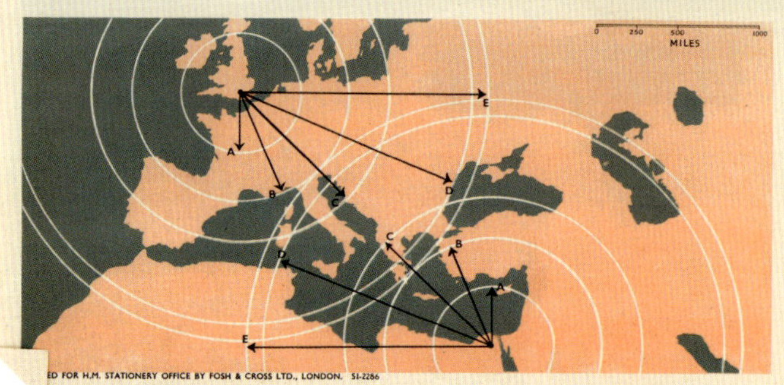

This "Aircraft of the RAF" poster shows the major types of aircraft then in service. By 1941 the Royal Air Force had introduced several new aircraft including its first four-engine heavy bomber, the Short Stirling. This was followed by the Handley Page Halifax and the rugged and lethal Bristol Beaufighter. (LOC)

With the Soviet entry into the war, both the United States and Britain began to supply their new ally with aircraft, tanks, trucks and essential raw materials. To help bolster Soviet morale, the RAF sent No. 151 Wing, equipped with Hurricane Mk I's to Vayenga, near Murmansk, during the autumn of 1941. This Air Ministry propaganda poster highlights their contribution to the war effort. (LOC)

A Canadian-built Lancaster X KB712/VL-R S (Smitty) of No. 419 Squadron Royal Canadian Air Force undergoes engine power checks at RAF Middleton St George in the spring of 1944. KB712 was shot down on the night of 28 October 1944 over Cologne. There were no survivors. (Author's Collection)

Ground crew work on Spitfire Mk XI, PM151 of No. 400 Squadron Royal Canadian Air Force at Petit-Brogel in Belgium in April 1945. This aircraft is painted in the standard Photo Reconnaissance Unit blue. Used for photo reconnaissance, the Mk XI was capable of 417 mph at 24,000 feet. (Author's Collection)

A line up of Royal Canadian Air Force Blackburn Shark Mk II's and their crews from No. 6 Torpedo Squadron, Vancouver, May 1939. The Shark was a British carrier-based torpedo bomber introduced in 1934. The RCAF purchased seven Mk II's and had a further 17 built by Boeing Aircraft of Canada. With the outbreak of war, the Sharks were re-equipped for anti-submarine and reconnaissance duties. (Author's Collection)

A No. 421 Squadron Royal Canadian Air Force Spitfire Mk XVIE undergoing maintenance in the spring of 1945. The Mk XVIE was armed with two 20 mm Hispano cannons and two .50-caliber machine guns. (Author's Collection)

A No. 440 Squadron Royal Canadian Air Force Typhoon "Pulverizer IV" taxis for takeoff armed with two general-purpose 1,000-pound bombs. The Typhoon suffered from many technical issues, including carbon monoxide fumes leaking into the cockpit. Pilots were instructed to always use their oxygen masks during start up and when flying the Typhoon. (Author's Collection)

Spitfire Mk XVIE's of No. 421 and No. 416 Royal Canadian Air Force newly arrived at their snow-covered base at B.56 Evere in Belgium in January 1945. The Mk XVI was powered by the American-built Packard Merlin 266 engine. (Author's Collection)

A Royal New Zealand Air Force Corsair Mk II loaded with a 1,000-pound bomb taxis out for another mission from the Piva airstrip, Bougainville. By late 1944 New Zealand had ten Corsair squadrons operational in the Pacific. They were primarily used for close air support of American, Australian and New Zealand troops fighting the Japanese in the Northern Solomon Islands. (RNZAFM)

Aerial photo of a Lockheed Ventura NZ4632 of No. 2 Squadron Royal New Zealand Air Force flying from Green Island on the way to bomb the Japanese naval and air base at Rabaul. Note the external bombload of two 500-pound bombs. New Zealand received 193 Venturas during the war. (RNZAFM)

This LeO-451 was damaged after a forced landing in June 1940. The LeO-451 was a four-seat medium bomber armed with two 7.5 mm machine guns and one 20 mm cannon and was capable of carrying 3,080-pounds of bombs. It was a good bomber, but just 94 were available for combat on 10 May 1940. (Author's Collection)

FRANCE

French Air Force

On 1 April 1933 the French Air Force became an independent arm of the French military. This was long after the formation of the Naval Air Force, which came into existence in 1912. At the conclusion of World War I, the French army and air force were arguably the most powerful in Europe, but the next ten years were a period of military stagnation. The horrendous loss of life during 1914–1918 seemed to create a siege mentality in France, the result of which was the construction of Maginot Line, a system of static forts and bunkers, along the Franco-German border. This absorbed much of the military budget, leaving little for the acquisition of new aircraft and the development of a coherent operational plan.

By 1937, the result of these policies were finally recognized. Although the air forces were equipped with substantial numbers of aircraft, most were obsolete at best. Political instability in the early 1930's led to the nationalization of the aviation industry, just as Germany reoccupied the Rhineland in 1936. Although France struggled to re-equip its air forces, it wasn't until the summer of 1940 that modern aircraft reached squadron service.

On 1 January 1937, the French Air Force had 795 fighters, of which 278 were regarded as "modern." The situation in terms of bombers was worse. Bombers like the Amoit 144 twin engine, of which 138 were delivered in 1937, were obsolete before it entered squadron service. Various planning studies were instigated, culminating in Plan V (5) in 1938. This called for the acquisition of 1,373 new-generation fighters, with the vast majority being 1,045 Morane Sauliner MS.406's. It was quickly realized that this ambitious plan was beyond the French aircraft industry, plagued as it was by inefficiencies and industrial unrest.

With Nazi Germany's increasing belligerence, the French, under conditions of the utmost secrecy, ordered large numbers of foreign aircraft, principally from the United States. Aircraft ordered included: the Curtiss Hawk H-75A-1 (172 on strength on 1 September 1939), 50 Curtiss SBC-4 dive-bombers, 449 Douglas DB-7's (export version of the A-20), 215 Martin Maryland 167 twin-engine bombers (140 delivered) and 20 Vought Vindicator SB2U navy dive-bombers.

On 1 September 1939 the French Air Force had 1,115 fighters in its inventory with 825 ready for combat along with 825 bombers. The Naval Air Force had approximately 1,000 aircraft, which included fighters, bombers, dive-bombers, torpedo bombers and patrol aircraft.

Combat Aircraft Available September 1939
Fighters: 1,115
Bombers: 825
Maritime Patrol Reconnaissance: 153

FRANCE

A Breguet Br.521 flying boat seen here at Brest harbor shortly after the fall of France, June 1940. The Br.521 was a long-range reconnaissance flying boat that entered service in 1935. From the beginning of hostilities, Br.521's flew both Atlantic and Mediterranean patrols. After the fall of France, a small number served with the Vichy Air Force in Algeria. (Author's Collection)

A Curtiss Hawk H-75C being prepared for its next mission in May 1940. The German invasion of France began at 03:53 hours on 10 May 1940. By the end of the day French Air Force fighters scored 70 confirmed victories, the majority by the H-75 equipped squadrons. (Author's Collection)

The Germans were not the only ones to use dive-bombers at the beginning of the war. During the Battle of France, two squadrons of Lorie-Nieuport LN-411 dive-bombers and two equipped with Chance-Vought V-156F's from the *Aeronavale* rose to the challenge, but losses were heavy with limited results. German troops inspect an LN-411 seen here after suffering a belly landing, May 1940. (Author's Collection)

A Dewoitine D.520 of Escadrille GC I/3 in 1940. The D.520 was easily the best French fighter available at the time of the German invasion of France on 10 May, but just one squadron was operational. Four more squadrons would join the fight before the armistice was signed on 25 June 1940. (Author's Collection)

Four Amiot-143 bombers flying in formation. The 143 was a high-wing, twin-engine monoplane design. It was a bulky-looking aircraft that did not have enough armor, speed or combat radius to make it an effective bomber. (Author's Collection)

The Farman F.221 was a four-engine heavy day-night bomber. About 80 of the large Farman F.220 series bombers were produced for the French Air Force and Navy prior to World War II. They saw little combat during the German invasion, and after the armistice they were moved to North Africa and served as transports for the Vichy Air Force. (Author's Collection)

This MS.406 was one of the many French aircraft damaged or destroyed during early Luftwaffe attacks on Allied airfields on 10 May 1940. There were 573 Morane Saulnier MS.406's on strength at the beginning of the war, more than any other French fighter. It was a reliable aircraft with pleasant characteristics but was outclassed by the better armed and faster German Bf 109E. (Author's Collection)

A Bloch MB-152 fighter after a landing mishap during the Battle of France in May 1940. It was just entering service in quantity in the spring of 1940. Despite its heavy armament of two long-barrelled 20 mm cannons and two 7.5 mm machine guns, the Bloch proved a disappointment as it was slower than the Bf 109, less maneuverable and underpowered. (Author's Collection)

Two Curtiss Hawk H-75 of No. 99 Squadron GC 1/4 in the spring of 1940. French Hawks were armed with four 7.5 mm FN Browning machine guns. While making up only 12.6 percent of the French Air Force single-seater fighter force, the H-75 accounted for almost a third of the air-to-air kills during the 1940 Battle of France. (Author's Collection)

The Caudron-CR-714 fighter was an attempt by the French to produce a lightweight fighter. Constructed of wood and powered by a 450-horsepower Renault air-cooled 12-cylinder engine, it had a top speed of 302 mph at 13,120 feet. Its poor performance compared to other contemporary fighters resulted in only 84 aircraft being built. During the Battle of France, Polish volunteer pilots used the CR-714's in combat, shooting down eight Luftwaffe aircraft with the loss of four pilots. (Author's Collection)

A Spitfire Mk IX of Fighter Group 2/7 attached to the U.S. First Tactical Air Force is seen here taxing out in snow and slush at Luxeuil, Belgium, in the winter of 1944–1945. (Author's Collection)

FRANCE

Free French Air Force

On 18 June 1940, just days before the Battle of France came to an end, Charles de Gaulle, an unknown French army general, announced on BBC radio, "the war is not lost." Seven days later the first three French pilots had flown to join de Gaulle and created the embryonic Free French Air Force.

Unlike the citizens of all of the other occupied countries, whose legitimate governments fled to England and supported their resistance movements, the French were caught in a bind. French pilots and ground crew were strongly discouraged from joining any Allied air force. Many who served in the Free French Air Force had a Vichy death sentence hanging over their heads for years.

A transition training camp was set up at Odiham in England, where French pilots and ground crew began re-training for service in the Royal Air Force. By August 1940 the first bomber squadron was formed. By the end of 1941 there were relatively few Frenchmen who opted to join the Free French Air Force, but there was still a base from which to begin the training of totally new squadrons. At the end of 1941 the Free French Air Force had just 186 pilots and 17 navigators. The first French squadron, GCIV/2 *Il de France*, known as No. 340 Squadron RAF, formed on 7 November 1941, flying Spitfire Mk V's. At the same time a small number of pilots headed east and joined the Soviet Air Force. There they formed the most famous Free French fighter Squadron, *Normandie-Niemen*.

This bomber and reconnaissance Bloch MB 131 was captured by the Germans after the fall of France in June 1940. The MB 131 stood in sharp contrast to the rather box-like and unattractive bombers the French were producing in the 1930s. The MB 131 was sleek with well-contoured lines, but by 1940 it was obsolete and suffered heavy losses in combat. (Author's Collection)

Blenheim Mk IV's of the Free French Air Force, clearly showing the Cross of Lorraine, operated as part of No. 320 Squadron RAF (Groupe Lorraine), based in Aleppo, Damascus, Syria, from 1940 to 1943. (Author's Collection)

A flight of Hawker Hurricane Mk I's of the Free French Air Force in 1943. The Hurricanes, like all Free French aircraft, sported the Cross of Lorraine on the fuselage and wings, instead of the red, white and blue roundel used by those aircraft flying for the Vichy French Air Force. (Author's Collection)

This Northrop N-3PB Nomad of No. 330 (Norwegian) Squadron Royal Air Force was part of Coastal Command based in Iceland. The Nomad was powered by a Wright GR-1820 air-cooled 1,200-horsepower radial engine. Top speed was 257 mph at sea level with a useful range of 1,000 miles. (Author's Collection)

NORWAY

Norwegian Army Air Service, Royal Norwegian Navy Air Service

Prior to the outbreak of war, the Norwegian air forces were considered some of the smallest in Europe. With war imminent, the Norwegians procured 12 British Gloster Gladiator fighters and six German Heinkel He 115A-2 floatplanes. The He 115 had a good reputation for strength, reliability, good armament and all-round versatility and was used extensively during the battle for Norway. Three Norwegian He 115A-2's and a captured Luftwaffe B-1 were flown to Scotland and continued flying until they were destroyed or ran out of spare parts.

To modernize its fighter fleet, 24 Curtiss H-75 Hawks were ordered from the United States, with 19 being delivered, but not operational, at the time of the German invasion on 9 April 1940. The second order of 26 H-75's was diverted to Canada, where they were used to train Norwegian pilots at what was called "Little Norway" on Toronto's Island Airport. The Northrop N-3PB Nomad single engine maritime floatplane was also ordered from the United States but was delivered straight to Britain after the fall of Norway. Eighteen Nomads were used to equip No. 330 (Norwegian) Squadron RAF and operated out of Iceland until 1943.

A Norwegian Army Air Service Gloster Gladiator fighter being inspected by a crowd of civilians after an emergency landing on the ice on the Mjøsa on 9 April 1940. This plane was one of seven belonging to the Fighter Wing stationed at Fornebu at the time of the German invasion. (Author's Collection)

Combat Aircraft Available April 1940
Fighters: 12
Maritime Patrol: 6

The Fokker T.V bomber was powered by two 925-horsepower Bristol Pegasus XXVI radial engines, had a bomb payload of 2,205 pounds and was armed with four 7.9 mm FN Browning defensive machine guns. The aircraft's primary weapon was a 20 mm Solothurn cannon mounted in the nose. (AAM)

NETHERLANDS

Dutch Air Force

The Dutch, who knew their neutrality held little influence with the Germans, relied on their domestic industry to produce fighters, bombers and maritime aircraft. Some of their designs were the equal of British and French aircraft. The Fokker T.V twin-engine bomber had a top speed of 264 mph with a bombload of 2,205 pounds. Sixteen were ordered in 1937.

Their most advanced aircraft was the Fokker G.I *Jachtkruiser*, a revolutionary design that was a domestic and international sensation when unveiled at the Air Show in Paris in November 1936. Powered by two Bristol Mercury engines, the G.I was a heavy fighter/bomber armed with eight 7.9 mm FN Browning machine guns and one rear gun. After testing revealed its impressive performance, 36 G.1A's were ordered in 1937. At the outbreak of war, the Dutch were equipped with 176 aircraft which included 16 Fokker T.V bombers, 36 Fokker D.XXI fighters, 35 Fokker G.1A's, seven Fokker D.XVII fighters, 11 Douglas DB-8A/3N light bombers, 20 Fokker C.X light bombers, 33 Fokker C.V reconnaissance aircraft along with 101 floatplanes and trainers from the Royal Dutch Naval Service.

Even after their defeat by the Germans, the Dutch armed forces continued to exist, but on the other side of the world. In Indonesia, then known as the Netherland East Indies, the Dutch had two colonial air forces: the Royal Netherlands Indies Army Air Force and the Royal Netherlands Naval Air Service. The two forces were equipped with a mix of Dutch, American and German aircraft. In December 1941 the Naval Air Service had 33 Dornier Do 24 flying boats, 35 Consolidated Catalina flying boats and six Fokker T-IV floatplanes. The Army Air Force had 83 Glenn Martin B-10 bombers, 71 Brewster B-339 fighters, 15 Curtiss Wright W21 fighters and 17 Curtiss Hawk 75A fighters.

Combat Aircraft Available Europe May 1940
Fighters: 78
Bombers: 47
Reconnaissance: 33

Combat Aircraft Available Indonesia December 1941
Fighters: 103
Bombers: 83
Maritime Patrol: 74

NETHERLANDS

The Fokker production line near Amsterdam shows a mix of aircraft including the T.V bomber and the D.XXI fighter. The D.XXI in the foreground was powered by an 840-horsepower Bristol Mercury VIII radial engine and was armed with four 7.9 mm FN Browning machine guns in its wings. (AAM)

This DB-8A/3N from the 3rd Fighter Squadron was shot down on the first day of the German invasion, 10 May 1940, at Ockenburg. The Douglas DB-8A/3N was the export version of the Northrop A-17A ground-attack aircraft. It was the only foreign aircraft in Dutch service at the outbreak of the war. Prior to the German invasion, the decision was made to use the DB-8A/3N in the fighter role. It was a tragic mistake. On 10 May, of the 12 aircraft ready for combat, seven were shot down, two crash landed, two landed safely and one was destroyed on the ground, but they did manage to shoot down two Luftwaffe Ju 52 transports. (AAM)

A Fokker D.XXI with a G.1A in the background. The D.XXI had fixed landing gear but had a respectable maximum speed. Its mixed welded steel tube, wood and fabric construction made it highly maneuverable. (AAM)

The production version of the Fokker G.1A had a large wing with a small fuselage in the center and twin tail booms. It was powered by two 800-horsepower Bristol Mercury VIII radial engines, similar to those used on the D.XXI. (AAM)

These spoils of war were captured by German forces in May 1940: a Fokker D.XXI, Douglas DB-8A/3N and G.1A. Short of fighters to meet the German invasion, the Dutch decided to bolster their force by using their DB-8A/3N light bombers as fighters. The results were disappointing with seven being shot down on the first day. (AAM)

A Fokker C.XIV in the foreground and T.VIII floatplane are shown here flying in formation. The Fokker C.XIV was a two-seat seaplane used as a trainer and reconnaissance aircraft; 24 were in service at the outbreak of the war. The Fokker T.VIII was a twin-engine torpedo bomber and reconnaissance aircraft. Nine T.VIII's escaped to Britian after the fall of the Netherlands and formed the nucleus of No. 320 (Netherlands) Squadron, Royal Air Force Coastal Command. (AAM)

Two factory-fresh Glenn Martin 139's (B-10) bombers in Dutch colors in May 1940. In the Dutch East Indies. The Dutch Government had procured 120 Glenn Martin 139's prior to the outbreak of war in the Pacific. At the time of the Japanese attack on 7 December 1941, the Royal Netherlands East Indies Army Air Force had 90 Glenn Martins 139's operational. (AAM)

The Royal Netherlands East Indies Army Air Force was one of the few air forces to use the rarely mentioned Curtiss-Wright CW 22 single-seat fighter. Here, a lineup of CW 21B's await inspection at Andir Airfield, Bandung, Java. Powered by a 420-horsepower Wright R-975-28 Whirlwind radial engine, it made its first flight in 1940. The Dutch ordered 86 aircraft, but 25 were diverted in transit to Australia in 1941 and confiscated by the U.S. Army Air Force. (AAM)

The Brewster Buffalo F2A's ordered by the Dutch were given the export designation B-339C and D. Of the 92 Brewster Buffalos ordered, only 67 were delivered in time to see combat against the Japanese invasion of the Dutch East Indies. Some crated Buffalos were aboard a Dutch freighter that reached Tjilatjap, Java, in early March of 1942 but could not be unloaded. These Buffalos were handed over to the U.S. Army Air Force in Australia. During three months of action against the Japanese, Dutch Buffalo pilots claimed 55 enemy aircraft shot down and suffered a loss of 30 Buffalos in the air, 15 on the ground and 15 to accidents. (AAM)

A Dornier Do 24 of the Royal Netherlands Naval Air Service in flight on the way to Fiji. During the three-month campaign against the Japanese that began in December 1941, the 37 Do 24's on strength played a vital role. On 17 December 1941, the Japanese destroyer *Shinonome* was sunk by a single Do 24. (RNZAFM)

A Gladiator Mk I runs up its engine prior to takeoff. On the morning of the German attack on Belgium, 10 May 1940, 14 Gladiators were ready for combat, but during a low-level attack by Luftwaffe Do 17's, most were destroyed on the ground. By the end of 11 May, the remaining six Gladiators were either shot down or destroyed on the ground. (Daniel Brackx)

BELGIUM

Belgium Army Air Service

As the approach of war became more apparent, the situation for Belgium was similar to that of the Netherlands. Being a neutral country, it hoped that war with Hitler could be avoided, but Germany had other plans. Up to 1935 the backbone of the Belgium Air Force was the Fairey Fox light bomber/fighter, of which they had 100 along with 28 domestically produced Renard R.31 parasol-wing observation aircraft. To bolster its air force, 25 Fairey Firefly IIM, 22 Gloster Gladiators, both biplane fighters, and 20 Hurricane Mk I fighters along with 16 Fairey Battle Mk I light bombers were ordered from Britain. The Belgians also acquired the license to produce an additional 80 Hurricanes, but only three were built before the German invasion began on 10 May 1940.

The Hurricane Mk I's, the most modern fighter in the Belgium Air Force, were entirely fabric covered and had no armor plate or bullet-resistant windscreens. Powered by a Merlin engine developing 1,030 horsepower and equipped with a Watts fixed-pitch two-blade airscrew, it had a top speed of 318 mph at 17,400 feet. In December 1939 Belgium signed a contract for 40 Brewster B-339B Buffalo fighters, a de-navalized version of the U.S. Navy F2A-1 powered by a Wright Cyclone R-1820-34 engine of 1,100 horsepower. The first B-339B was shipped to Belgium on 27 April 1940 and was the only example delivered before the German invasion with the rest of the order being diverted to Britain. In December 1939 an additional 40 Fiat CR.42 fighters were purchased from Italy shortly after the outbreak of war. By the time of the German invasion, 34 CR.42's had been delivered. Although obsolete at the time of the German invasion, the CR. 42 was the most successful Belgian fighter, claiming five aerial victories and six probable victories against the loss of only two Fiats in aerial combat.

This Brewster Model 339 B, in Belgian markings, was one of 40 ordered by the Belgium Air Force prior to the outbreak of war. Just one aircraft made it to the country before Belgium was overrun by the Germans. With a top speed of 323 mph at 16,500 feet and armed with four .50-caliber machine guns, it was just as fast as the Hawker Hurricane Mk I but had better armament. (NASM)

Combat Aircraft Available May 1940
Fighters: 101
Bombers: 116

BELGIUM

Although considered obsolete in 1940 and despite technical problems with the synchronizing gear and ammunition, the Fiat CR.42 was the most successful Belgian fighter during its short war, claiming five aerial victories and six probable victories with the loss of only two CR.42's in aerial combat. (Daniel Brackx)

The Belgium Battles, like their Royal Air Force counterparts, suffered horrendous losses during the German invasion of the Low Countries and France in May 1940. Slow, poorly armed and able to carry only a modest bombload, they were easy targets for Luftwaffe fighters and flak. During the ill-fated attack on the Albert Canal bridges, six out of the nine attacking Battles were shot down and there was no damage to the bridges. (Daniel Brackx)

A lineup of RHAF PZL P.24 fighters at Sedes Air Base, Greece, prior to the outbreak of war. The P.24 was powered the 970-horsepower Gnome-Rhone 14N-07 engine and was armed with four 7.7 mm machine guns. (Author's Collection)

GREECE

Royal Hellenic Air Force (RHAF)

The Royal Hellenic Air Force was established in 1911 and was one of the first air forces to cooperate with the navy in the use of aircraft. As a small country, Greece did not have a significant aircraft industry of its own and had to rely on aircraft from abroad. The first large purchase occurred in 1922, when 25 Gloster Mk VI Nighthawks were purchased from Britain. In 1931 more aircraft were ordered, with 30 Breguet XIX's and 30 Potez 30's coming from France and six Hawker Horsley II's and six Fairey IIIF seaplanes coming from Britain.

Like many other countries in Europe, Greece's rearmament efforts in the mid-1930s were still far from complete at the start of the war. At the end of 1936 the Royal Hellenic Air Force ordered 24 gull-winged PZL P.24 fighters from Poland. Twenty-four Marcel Bloch MB.151 French fighters were ordered in 1939, but only nine were delivered by June 1940. Bombers included 9 to 12 British Bristol Blenheim Mk IV's ordered in 1937, 11 Fairey Battle Mk I's delivered in March 1940, and 12 Avro Anson Mk I's. Aircraft from Germany included 12 Dornier Do 22G floatplanes and 16 Henschel Hs 126 army cooperation aircraft. In October 1940 the Royal Hellenic Air Force fielded some 150 aircraft: 24 PZL P.24's, nine Bloch MB 151 fighters, eight Potez 63's, 11 Bristol Blenheim Mk IV's, 10 Fairey Battle Mk I bombers and 35 Henschel Hs 126's.

Combat Aircraft Available October 1940

Fighters: 33
Bombers: 29
Army Cooperation: 35

GREECE

The Italian invasion of Greece began on 28 October 1940 and lasted until 23 April 1941. At the time of the invasion the Royal Hellenic Air Force was small, but its serviceability rates were high. Supporting the Greek army in the reconnaissance and bombing role were approximately 16 Henschel He 126's. Here ground crew pose in front of their hastily camouflaged He 126 somewhere in Albania. (Author's Collection)

A Blenheim Mk IV bomber on Trikala Airstrip, Greece, in October 1940. At the time of the Italian invasion the Greek bomber force consisted of 12 Blenheim Mk IV's and 12 single-engine Fairey Battle Mk I's. (Author's Collection)

Two Zmaj Fizir FP-2 advanced trainers burn after being attacked by Luftwaffe fighters. Luftwaffe bombers and fighters caught and destroyed many Yugoslavian aircraft on the ground during the early hours of their attack. The FP-2 two-seater was powered by an air-cooled, seven-cylinder radial engine, the Gnome-Rhone K-7 308 kW. (Author's Collection)

YUGOSLAVIA

Royal Yugoslavian Air Force (RYAF)

Yugoslavia was one of the few countries that was able to acquire a good selection of modern foreign-built bombers and fighters from the mid-1930s to 1941. After the defeat of the central powers in World War I, the geopolitical map in Europe changed drastically. In 1929 the Kingdom of Yugoslavia was formed out of the ashes of the Kingdoms of Slovenia, Croatia and Serbia.

Beginning in 1932, the Royal Yugoslavian Air Force was equipped with older biplane fighters and bombers of French origin, with 150 Breguet biplane attack aircraft and 40 Potez 25 reconnaissance aircraft built under license. On 19 September 1935 the Yugoslavians ordered 10 Hawker Fury II fighters from the British along with the license to build the Fury. In November 1937 the domestic Ikarus company was given a contract for 12 high-wing IK-2 fighters, Yugoslavia's first indigenous fighter. The IK-2 had a respectable top speed of 280 mph and was armed with one 20 mm cannon and two 7.7 mm machine guns. The most modern domestically produced fighter was the Rogozarski IK-3 monoplane fighter. With a top speed of 325 mph and armed with a single 20 mm Oerlikon cannon and two 7.92 mm Browning FN machine guns, the IK-3 was a big improvement over the IK-2. Because too many parts had to be imported from across worn-torn Europe, just 12 aircraft were ordered in 1939.

Prior to the outbreak of war, the Royal Yugoslavian Air Force was able to order and license-build a good number of modern aircraft, including: 73 Bf 109E-3's, 47 Hawker Hurricane Mk I fighters, 30 Hawker Fury II's, 61 Bristol Blenheim Mk I's, 69 Dornier Do 17Z's and 40 Savioa-Marchetti SM.79K bombers. An impressive number given the circumstances.

Combat Aircraft Available April 1941
Fighters: 174
Bombers: 170

YUGOSLAVIA

A Yugoslavian Dornier Do 17K. Despite a valiant fight against the Luftwaffe, the outnumbered and outgunned Royal Yugoslavian Air Force saw many of its aircraft either destroyed or captured. A small number of Do 17K's escaped to Greece at the end of the conflict. (Author's Collection)

On 6 April 1941, Luftwaffe units based in Bulgaria attacked Yugoslavia. After Yugoslav Prime Minister Cvetković signed the Tripartite Pact, his regime was overthrown by a military coup. Italy had demanded Germany invade Yugoslavia to help them in their disastrous campaign to conquer Greece. At the time, the Royal Yugoslavian Air Force was well-equipped and included ten of the indigenous-built and designed Ikarus IK-2 fighters. Seen here, the IK-2 was a single-seat high wing fighter with a top speed of 270 mph at 16,000 feet. (Author's Collection)

A lineup of Royal Yugoslavian Air Force Bf 109E-3's in 1941. At the time of the German invasion of Yugoslavia, the Yugoslavian Air Force had 64 or 65 Bf 109E-3's that were operational. During the short 11-day campaign, Yugoslavian fighters and anti-aircraft defenses shot down 90 to 100 Luftwaffe aircraft. (Author's Collection)

Yugoslavia's best-built fighter was the Ikarus IK-3. Few in number, there were just 12; it had the same performance as the Bf 109E-3. IK-3 pilots claimed 11 Luftwaffe aircraft shot down during 11 days of combat. (Author's Collection)

The Petlyakov Pe-8 was designed before the war and was the only modern Soviet heavy four-engine bomber to see service the during the war with Germany. This aircraft is being serviced at Bolling Field, Washington, D.C., in 1942. It had brought Soviet Foreign Minister Vyacheslav Molotov to the United States for meetings with President Roosevelt. The flight from Moscow required transiting German-controlled airspace and a stop in London before proceding to Washington. (USNHHC)

SOVIET UNION

Soviet Air Force

Unlike the French, the Soviet aircraft industry had no real problems producing aircraft in quantity. What it lacked was modern aircraft. In June 1941 Soviet Air Force aircraft outnumbered the Luftwaffe by a wide margin, with 7,133 aircraft in the five special military districts on the border plus 1,339 bombers controlled by Long Range Aviation and another 1,445 controlled by the Baltic and Black Seas fleets. It was the world's largest air force.

Prior to the outbreak of war, the Soviet Union, like the rest of Europe, had embarked on a modernization and expansion program. Unfortunately for the Soviets, and like the Italians, they began expansion too early. During the mid-1930s the Soviets and Italy were producing some of the best combat aircraft in the world, including the four-engine TB-3 long-range bomber, twin-engine Tupolev SB-2 fast bomber, maneuverable fighters like the Polikarpov I-15, 1-153 biplane fighters and the 1-16, the first low-wing monoplane fighter with cannon armament and retractable landing gear.

After initial success during the Spanish Civil War (1936–1939), Soviet fighters and bombers were soon outclassed by Germany's Condor Legion and their more modern Heinkel He 111's, Junkers Ju 87's and Messerschmitt Bf 109's. The massive purges of the Soviet Armed Forces before the war and the abject failure of Soviet air power against the vastly outnumbered Finnish Air Force during the Winter War in 1939 resulted in a desperate attempt to expand, rearm and modernize the air force. The turmoil and confusion that followed resulted in a force short of modern aircraft, training, logistics and leadership. As a result, just ten percent of the fighter force at the time of the German attack in 1941 was equipped with new-generation aircraft like the LaGG-3, Yak-1 and MiG-3.

Combat Aircraft Available June 1941
Fighters: 11,500
Bombers: 8,400
Ground Attack: 249

SOVIET UNION

This partially camouflaged Soviet Polikarpov I-153 was captured by the Finns on 25 June 1941. This aircraft was later used against the Soviets. The Finnish Air Force made significant use of captured Soviet aircraft during the Winter War, 1939–1940, and the Continuation War, 1941–1944. (SA-Kuva)

This Lavochkin LaGG-3 was shot down in Finland in 1941. Made of plastic-impregnated wood skinned with stressed Bakelite plywood, the LaGG-3 was initially powered by a single 1,100-horsepower Klimov M-105P 12-cylinder liquid-cooled engine that gave it a top speed of 366 mph. Compared to the German Bf 109E/F, Soviet pilots considered the LaGG-3 to be slower, heavier and less maneuverable. (SA-Kuva)

This German soldier is standing on a captured Tupolev SB-2 during Operation *Barbarossa* in 1941. At the outbreak of the war in September 1939, the SB-2 was not only the most common bomber in Soviet service, but it was also likely the most numerous bomber in the world. (Author's Collection)

A Tupolev SB-2 aircraft in flight. The SB-2 first entered combat with Soviet aircrews during the Spanish Civil War (1936–1939); it later operated successfully and shocked Japanese pilots flying the Nakajima Ki-27 "Nate" fighter during the brief Sino-Japanese War in December 1937. (RNZAFM)

These three Polikarpov I-16's of 4GvIAP are part of the Soviet Baltic Fleet. The aircraft had insulated engine covers in place between sorties because of the cold. On the eve of Operation *Barbarossa*, the I-16 made up over 65 percent of the entire Soviet fighter inventory. (Author's Collection)

An I-16 shot down during the early days of Operation *Barbarossa* on 22 June 1941. In the first 48 hours of the German invasion, Soviet I-16 units were key targets for Luftwaffe bombers and fighter bombers, resulting in 937 I-16's destroyed in the air and on the ground out of 1,635 that existed on 21 June. (Author's Collection)

Petlyakov Pe-2's of the 3rd Bomber Air Corps hit German targets near Bobruisk, Belarus, on the Belorussian Front in late 1944. The Pe-2 was considered to be one of the best attack aircraft of the war. It was fast, versatile, maneuverable and a highly accurate dive-bomber. (Author's Collection)

This Yakovlev Yak-1 along with the Mikoyan MiG-3 and Lavochkin LaGG-3 were the next generation of modern Soviet fighters, but they had not yet reached frontline units in significant numbers in 1941. By 22 June 1941, just 2,030 of these new types of fighters had been built. (Author's Collection)

These Douglas A-20's, armed with torpedoes, are part of the Soviet Baltic Fleet in September 1944. The largest single user of the A-20 series was the Soviet Air Force, which received over 3,000 aircraft from the United States under the Lend Lease agreement. (Author's Collection)

Roughly equal to the Heinkel He 111 in terms of performance and bombload, the Ilyushin Il-4 was the first Soviet bomber to raid Berlin in August 1941. Between 7 August and 14 September, the Soviet Air Force launched 86 individual sorties with 33 aircraft reaching Berlin. Some 72,900 pounds of bombs were dropped, and 17 aircraft were lost. Here, an Il-4 is cleared for takeoff in the spring of 1945. (USNHHC)

Three Tupolev Tu-2's of the 334th Bomber Air Division head to their target on the Russian front. The Tu-2 did not enter service until November 1944 and saw its final action against the Japanese Kwantung Army in August 1945. The Tu-2 proved to be one of the most effective bombers of the war due to its excellent design and performance. (Gennady Sloutski)

In this photograph, Ilyushin DB-3T crew members prepare for their next mission. The DB-3 proved vulnerable to enemy fighters, and, as a result, the upgraded Ilyushin Il-4 version was produced with improved performance and up gunned to carry one 20 mm gun in the nose and two 12.7 mm machine guns in the dorsal and ventral positions. (Author's Collection)

During the war, the United States and Great Britain supplied the Soviets with large quantities of fighters. The principal British aircraft supplied were the Spitfire Mk V's, Mk IX's and Hurricanes. These Mk V's are being serviced at Kuban, Russia, in 1943. The Soviets received a total of 1,338 Spitfire V's and Mk IX's during the war. (Author's Collection)

The Soviets received 2,952 Hawker Hurricanes like this one from Great Britain but were not impressed with the Hurricane's eight .303-inch machine guns. To increase the aircraft's firepower, most Hurricanes were modified to carry two ShVAK 20 mm cannons in their place, as seen here. (Author's Collection)

Three Ilyushing Il-4s return to base in July 1942. The Il-4 was used as a bomber but also saw service as a transport aircraft, glider tug and strategic reconnaissance aircraft. A total of 5,256 were built during the war. (USNHHC)

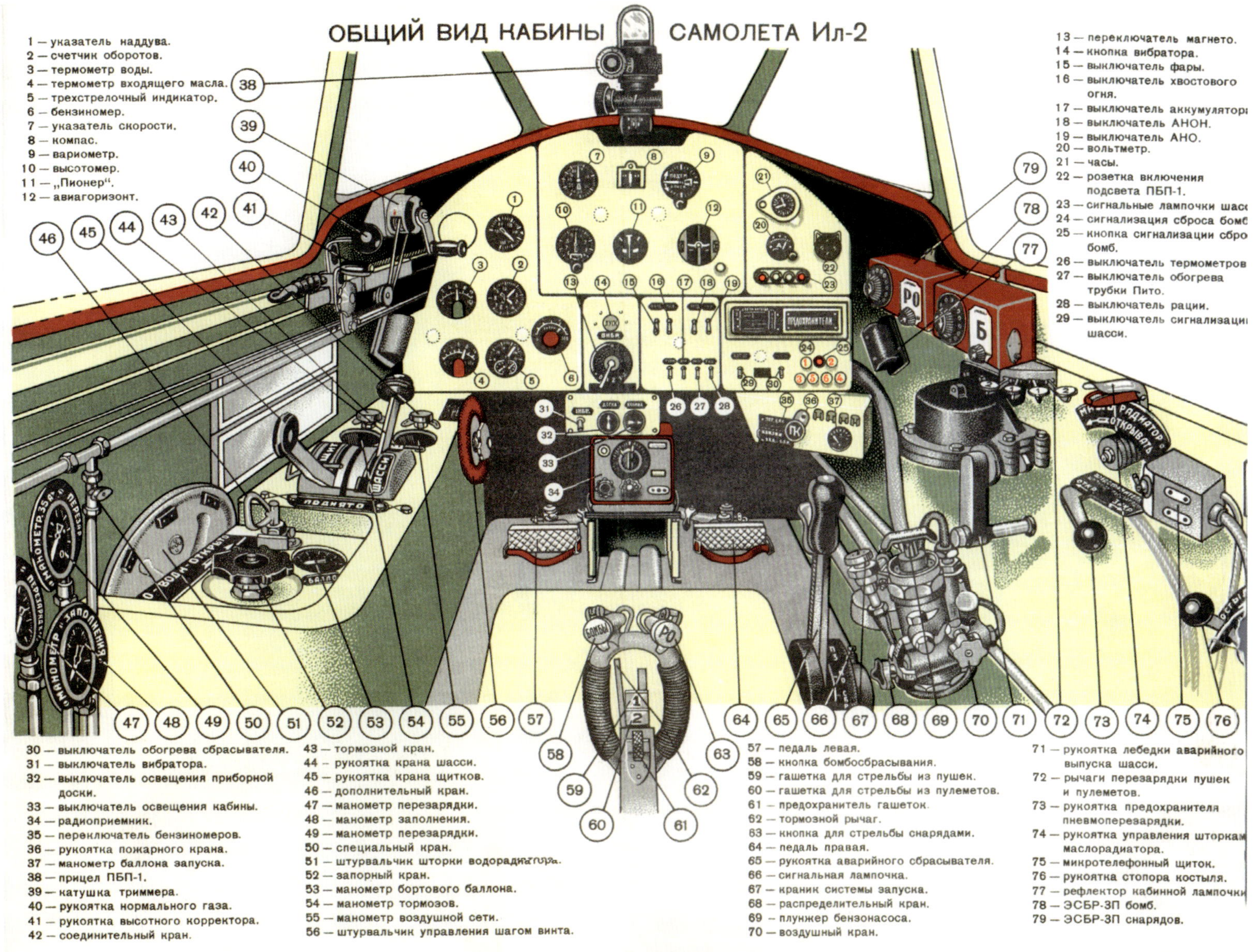

The cockpit of the Il-2 Shturmovik "Flying Tank" had a very clean and well-laid out design. It was also one of the most well-protected cockpits, surrounded by thick armor and bullet-resistant windscreen and canopy glass. As a ground-attack aircraft, the Il-2 could carry 2,640 pounds of bombs and had a range of 250 miles. (Author's Collection)

The Il-2 was one of most heavily armored ground-attack aircraft of the war. A heavy case-hardened one-piece armored tub surrounded the pilot. The back of the tub was sealed off by a 13 mm thick piece of armor plate. The engine was also surrounded by armor plate with a thickness of between 4 and 5 mm. The rear gunner was less fortunate; he had just a 6 mm plate to protect him from enemy fighters. (Author's Collection)

The Yak-9D was the first long-range version of the basic Yak-9 design. Introduced to Soviet operations in late 1943, the Yak-9 served as both a frontline fighter and fighter bomber. Its performance compared favorably to both the German Bf 109G and the Focke Wulf Fw 190-3/A-4, and it was well liked by its pilots. Total war production amounted to 16,700 aircraft. (Author's Collection)

These Yak-7A's under construction are powered by a 1,100-horsepower Klimov M-105 PA engine. The Yak-7's performance was similar to the Yak-9, with a maximum speed of 364 mph at 16,400 feet. Armament consisted of one 20 mm ShVAK cannon and two 7.62 mm ShKAS machine guns. (Author's Collection)

A formation of Petlyakov-Pe2's releases their bombs at medium altitude over the Karelian Isthmus in June 1944. Bombing from this height seldom had much success. The Soviets preferred low-level bomb strikes and dive-bombing attacks for better accuracy. (Author's Collection)

The Lavochkin La-7 entered service in January 1944 and was one of the finest Soviet fighters of the war. Basically, it was an aerodynamically refined version of the La-5. At low-level, the La-7 was capable of outrunning both the Bf 109G and Fw 190A. With a top speed of 423 mph, excellent climbing performance and greater range, it became the favored choice among leading Soviet aces. (Author's Collection)

Three Yakovlev Yak-9D's in the winter of 1945. Produced in larger numbers than any other Soviet fighter, the Yak-9 saw continuous action as a fighter and fighter bomber from October 1942 until the end of the war. (Author's Collection)

This Curtiss P-40 of the 18th Fighter Squadron is being refueled in the Aleutians in 1943. P-40's served on almost every front during the war and saw service with the British, Canadian, Australian, New Zealand, South African, Soviet, Chinese, Dutch and Brazilian Air Forces. (NARA)

UNITED STATES

U.S. Army Air Corps, U.S. Navy, U.S. Marine Corps

As Europe prepared for war, military aircraft production in the United States remained stagnant. Apart from an increase in foreign orders from the British, French, Chinese, Dutch and Finnish air forces, the American aircraft industry, which employed 36,000 workers, delivered just 900 aircraft to the U.S. Army Air Corps and U.S. Navy in 1938. In those days an order for 50 aircraft was considered enormous.

As the aircraft industry received foreign orders, the production picked up appreciably in 1939. Delivery rates were slow, however, and even with foreign orders, only 2,250 military aircraft were produced in the United States in 1939. As France was falling in May 1940, President Roosevelt called for the United States to increase its annual production of aircraft to 50,000 and to maintain a frontline strength of the same number of aircraft, with the Army Air Corps deploying 36,500 aircraft and the Navy 13,500.

Although production rates were slow, America was producing modern fighters and bombers. The Lockheed P-38 Lightning and Curtiss P-36 and P-40 fighters were in production along with heavy bombers like the Boeing B-17 and Consolidated B-24. The U.S. Navy had the Grumman F4F Wildcat fighter along with the Douglas SBD dive-bomber and the first prototype of the Chance Vought XF4U-1 fighter, which made its first flight in May 1940.

Roosevelt's plan was ambitious and faced many hurdles, but aircraft production began to rise with 6,000 airframes produced in 1940. When the United States entered World War II on 7 December 1941, the U.S. Army Air Corps was one of the smallest air forces in the world, with approximately 1,100 aircraft, which included 700 bombers of all types. The U.S. Navy's aircraft carriers counted 131 F4F Wildcat fighters, 108 Brewster F2A-3 Buffalos, 192 Douglas SBD dive-bombers, approximately 50 Vought SB2U-2 Vindcators and 99 Douglas TB-1 Devastator torpedo bombers.

Combat Aircraft Available December 1941

U.S. ARMY AIR CORPS

Fighters: 400

Bombers: 700

U.S. NAVY/MARINE CORPS

Fighters: 239

Dive-Bombers: 242

Torpedo Bombers: 99

Maritime/Patrol: 203 (Pacific Theatre)

UNITED STATES

During the Japanese attack on Pearl Harbor on 7 December 1941, 12 unarmed B-17C and E four-engine bombers arrived over Oahu after a long flight from California. Unaware of the events then unfolding at their destination, several of them were attacked. This B-17C/40-2049 was heavily damaged by Japanese fighters and crash landed. It was salvaged for spare parts. Only two B-17's were destroyed that day. (USNHHC)

A Grumman F4F-3 Wildcat of VF-3 from the USS *Yorktown* lands on CV-8 USS *Hornet* on 4 June 1942, during the Battle of Midway. By June, most F4F-3's had been replaced by the F4F-4 version, with folding wings and six .50-caliber machine guns. (NARA)

This 8 mm cine still frame shows a Seversky P-35 of the 17th Pursuit Squadron with Swedish markings at Clark Field in the Philippines in February 1941. In June 1940 the United States declared an arms embargo that prohibited the export of weapons to countries other than the United Kingdom. A Swedish order for 60 P-35's was taken over by the U.S. Air Force and 50 were sent to reinforce the U.S. Far East Air Force in the Philippines. (Author's Collection)

This 8 mm cine still frame image shows a Boeing P-26 from the 17th Pursuit Squadron in early 1941. At the time of the Japanese attack on Clarke Field on 7 December 1941, the U.S. Far East Air Force still had 12 of these obsolete fighters on strength. (Author's Collection)

The remains of a U.S. Marine Corps F4F Wildcat after another Japanese air attack on Henderson Field, Guadalcanal, in 1942. During the six-month Guadalcanal campaign, the U.S. Navy and Marine Wildcats provided the bulk of the fighter defense for the island and suffered a 20 percent loss rate. (NARA)

An engine run-up on a B-17E in preparation for a night flight. The B-17E served both in the Pacific and in Europe, with the first aircraft arriving in England in July 1942. These aircraft were armed with eight .50-caliber machine guns and a single .30-caliber machine gun in the nose. (Author's Collection)

The B-17G required a crew of 10 highly trained men: pilot, co-pilot, navigator, bombardier, radio operator, engineer and gunner, ball-turret gunner, two waist gunners and a tail gunner. A fully equipped B-17 and its crew was an extremely expensive endeavor. A B-17 cost $212, 632 in 1944, which is the equivalent of just over 2 million in today's dollars. Aircrew training took months (up to a year for pilots and navigators), whereas training for a rifle-carrying infantryman was measured in weeks. (NARA)

A factory-fresh Boeing B-17F in Burbank, California. The first F models were delivered by Boeing in late May 1942, with Douglas and Lockheed Vega deliveries following during the summer. By August the three plants combined were producing an average of 400 aircraft per month. (NARA)

This flight of 352nd Fighter Group P-51 Mustangs, the "Blue Nose Bastards of Bodney," escort Liberators of the 458th Bomb Group across the English Channel in mid-1944. The 352nd was one of the most successful fighter groups in the 8th Air Force, credited with destroying 800 enemy aircraft between 1943 and 1945. (NARA)

A Mosquito Mk XVI of the 25th Bomb Group (Recon). Demand for the Mosquito during the war was so great that only 200 reached the U.S. Army Air Force. With a top speed of 408 mph at 25,200 feet, the Germans found it extremely difficult to intercept the Mosquito, and it was the Allied aircraft they hated the most. (Author's Collection)

This Spitfire PR Mk XI of the 7th Photo Group is painted in British Photo Recon Unit blue. The Mk XI had a top speed of 422 mph. Unarmed, it relied on its speed and high-altitude performance to avoid interception. (Author's Collection)

Brazilian ground crew clean the guns on their P-47 in Italy in 1944. The 1st Brazilian Fighter Squadron (BFS) served with the U.S. 350th Fighter Group beginning in October 1944. By the end of the war, the 1st BFS had flown 445 missions, 2,550 individual sorties and 5,465 combat flight hours. (NARA)

This rare color photo, taken from the tail gunner's position, shows the B-17's of the 385th Bomb Group plowing through heavy flak over Germany in January 1945. The U.S. 8th and 15th Air Forces lost a combined total of 2,844 heavy bombers shot down by German flak. (Author's Collection)

The B-24 "Joisey Bounce" of the 330th Bomber Squadron flying in formation with three other B-24's. This aircraft was lost on 13 November 1943 on a mission to Bremen. Built in greater numbers than any other American four-engine bomber, the Liberator has often been overshadowed by the more famous B-17. While more demanding to fly than the B-17, the B-24 had superior range and carried a bigger bombload. (NARA)

These Lockheed P-38H's are part of the newly arrived 20th Fighter Group at Wittering, England, in December 1943. The 20th Fighter Group scored its first victory on 7 January 1944, when a German Bf 109 was destroyed in combat. (NARA)

This P-51D of the 3rd Scouting Force, equipped with two 108-gallon drop tanks, has the cockpit covered in the cold winter of 1944. Based at Womingfold, England, the unit was active from August 1944 until May 1945. (Little Friends)

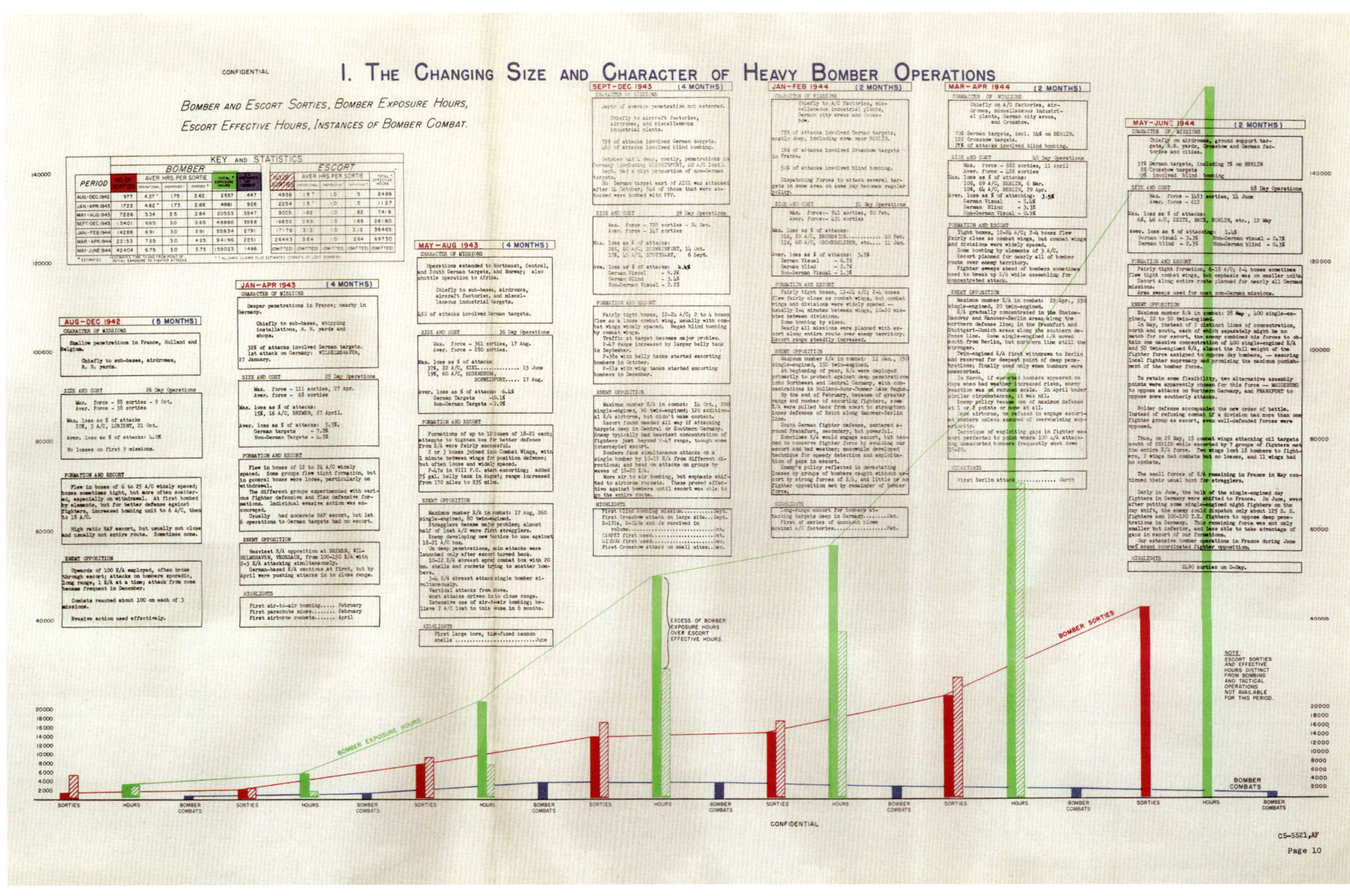

This "The Changing Size and Character of Heavy Bomber Operations" chart provides a concise graphic overview of the achievements of the 8th Air Force's bomber operations from August 1942 until June 1944. (Author's Collection)

CONFIDENTIAL

19-FREQUENCY, CAUSE AND LOCATION OF FIRES ON LOST BOMBERS

[BASED ON INFORMATION OBTAINED FROM 710 RETURNING CREW MEMBERS OF 302 HEAVY BOMBERS LOST FROM OCT. 1942 THROUGH JUNE 1944]

A. FREQUENCY OF FIRES ON LOST BOMBERS

1. 55 OF EVERY 100 BOMBERS LOST IN 1943 HAD FIRES

55 BOMBERS HAD FIRES

ON 40 BOMBERS FIRE WOULD HAVE CAUSED LOSS REGARDLESS OF OTHER DAMAGE — ON 15 BOMBERS FIRE WAS MINOR CAUSE OF LOSS — ON 45 BOMBERS THERE WERE NO FIRES

2. 44 OF EVERY 100 BOMBERS LOST IN 1944 HAD FIRES

44 BOMBERS HAD FIRES

ON 31 BOMBERS FIRE WOULD HAVE CAUSED LOSS REGARDLESS OF OTHER DAMAGE — ON 13 BOMBERS FIRE WAS MINOR CAUSE OF LOSS — ON 56 BOMBERS THERE WERE NO FIRES

B. CAUSE OF FIRES ON LOST BOMBERS

FIGHTERS AND FLAK TOGETHER ACCOUNT FOR OVER 90% OF ALL FIRES. FLAK CAUSES FIRE LESS FREQUENTLY THAN FIGHTERS, AND THE RELATIVE INCREASE IN FLAK AS A CAUSE OF LOSS LARGELY ACCOUNTS FOR THE DECREASE IN FIRES IN 1944.

FOR EXAMPLE: IN THOSE CASES WHERE THE LOSS WAS REPORTED AS BEING DUE SOLELY TO FLAK OR SOLELY TO FIGHTERS.

1. FLAK-CAUSED LOSSES INVOLVED FIRE LESS FREQUENTLY THAN FIGHTER-CAUSED LOSSES.

FOR EVERY 100 BOMBERS LOST SOLELY TO FLAK: 51 (NO FIRES) — 49 (HAD FIRES)

FOR EVERY 100 BOMBERS LOST SOLELY TO FIGHTERS: 33 (NO FIRES) — 67 (HAD FIRES)

2. FLAK-CAUSED LOSSES INCREASED SUBSTANTIALLY IN 1944 IN RELATION TO FIGHTER-CAUSED LOSSES.

FOR EVERY 100 BOMBERS REPORTED AS LOST TO FIGHTER OR FLAK ALONE

IN 1943 ONLY 27 WERE LOST TO FLAK ALONE — (LOST TO FLAK ALONE) 27 — (LOST TO FIGHTERS ALONE) 73

IN 1944 44 WERE LOST TO FLAK ALONE — (LOST TO FLAK ALONE) 44 — (LOST TO FIGHTERS ALONE) 56

C. LOCATION OF FIRES ON LOST BOMBERS

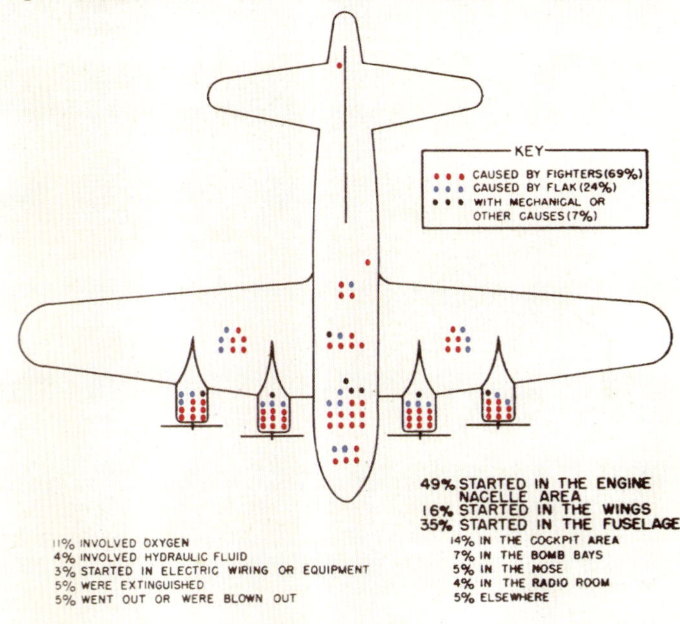

SUMMARY

1. ABOUT ONE IN EVERY TWO LOST BOMBERS GOES DOWN ON FIRE. (55%) IN 1943, 44% IN 1944)
2. ALMOST HALF OF ALL FIRES START IN THE ENGINE NACELLES, ONE THIRD IN THE FUSELAGE, ONE SIXTH IN THE WINGS.
3. NO NEW MEASURES TO PREVENT FIRES WERE TAKEN DURING THE PERIOD COVERED BY THIS STUDY.
4. THE DECREASE IN FIRE RATE BETWEEN 1943 AND 1944 IS PROBABLY DUE TO THE DECREASE IN FIGHTER-CAUSED LOSSES IN 1944 SINCE 2/3 OF BOMBERS LOST TO FIGHTERS HAVE FIRES, BUT ONLY 1/2 OF BOMBERS LOST TO FLAK HAVE FIRES.

C5-5521,F

This graphic illustration comes from a report entitled *An Evaluation of Defensive Measures Taken to Protect Heavy Bombers from Loss and Damage: Operational Analysis Section, November 1944*. It shows that one in every two bombers lost went down in flames, with almost half the loses being caused by engine fires due to damage by enemy fighters or flak. (Author's Collection)

B-17's flying over Kassel, Germany, under heavy flak in 1944. The 8th Air Force lost a total of 1,798 heavy bombers to flak. The 15th Air Force lost a further 1,046 heavy bombers. Another 54,539 8th Air Force and 11,954 15th Air Force bombers were damaged between December 1942 and April 1945. (NARA)

P-47Ds of the 63rd Fighter Squadron equipped with two 100-gallon drop tanks line up for takeoff in 1944. Later models of the P-47D with two such drop tanks had a range of 1,360 miles, making it more effective as an escort fighter capable of flying to Berlin and back. (Little Friends)

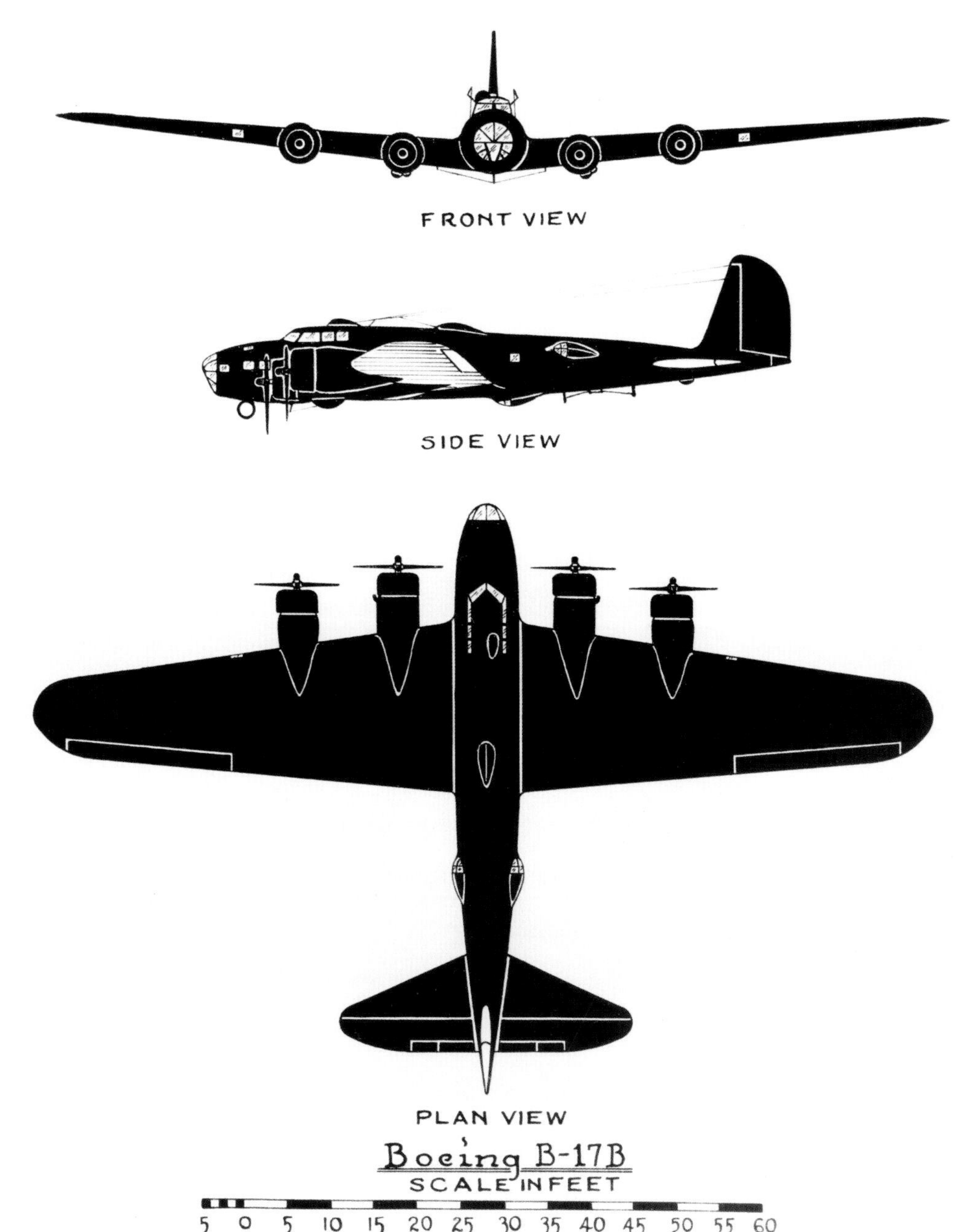

This aircraft identification poster shows the Boeing B-17B model "Flying Fortress." A total of 39 B-17's were built, with the first delivered in July 1939 to the U.S. Army Air Corps 2nd and 7th Bomb Groups. (LOC)

CONFIDENTIAL

14 - Attacks and Hits on B-17s and B-24s
JANUARY–MAY 1944

KEY: ATTACKS: 1 A/C SYMBOL EQUALS 2% OF TOTAL INSTANCES OF COMBAT
HITS: (SUCCESSFUL ATTACKS): 1 BURST SYMBOL EQUALS 2% OF TOTAL HITS

A–Distribution According To Direction Of Origin In Azimuth

B-17

Percentage Distribution Of 3585 Attacks And Of 441 Hits Whose Direction Could Be Determined.

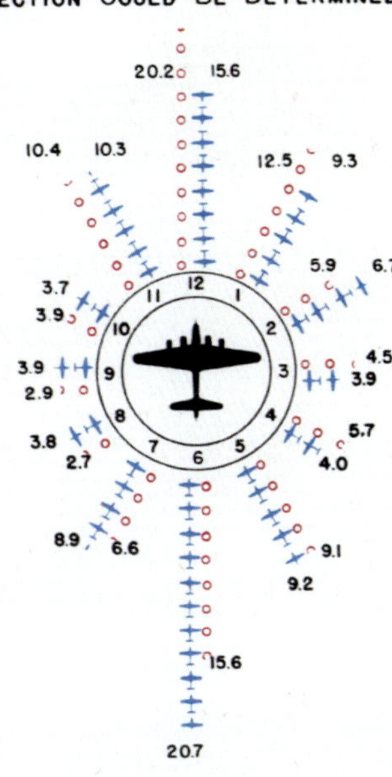

B-24

Percentage Distribution Of 1042 Attacks And Of 102 Hits Whose Direction Could Be Determined.

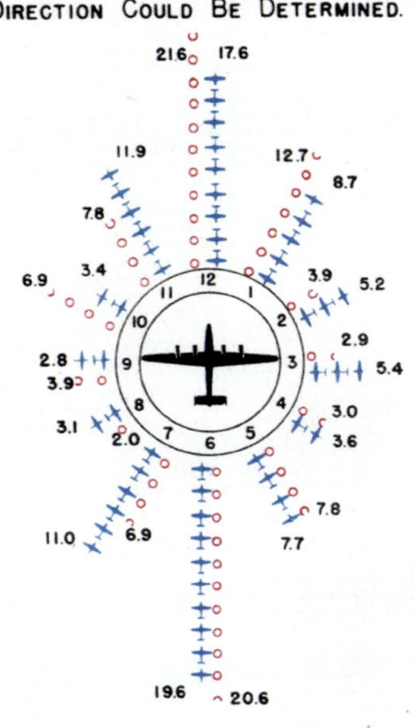

B– Distribution According To Direction Of Origin In Zenith

B-17

Percentage Distribution Of 3585 Attacks And Of 251 Hits Whose Direction Could Be Determined.

B-24

Percentage Distribution Of 1042 Attacks And Of 79 Hits Whose Direction Could Be Determined.

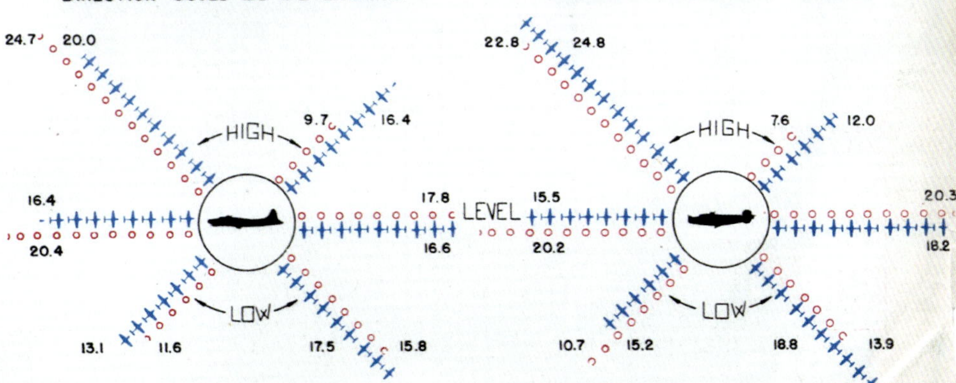

CONFIDENTIAL
-41-
C5-5521,AF

Luftwaffe fighter tactics against American bombers varied throughout the 1942–1945 bombing campaign. This graphic entitled "Attacks and Hits on B-17s and B-24s January–May 1944" shows the majority of Luftwaffe fighter attacks and hits came from the front (12 o'clock) position and rear (6 o'clock) position. Frontal fighter attacks required the most skill, due the high combined closing speeds of the fighter and bomber. (Author's Collection)

P-51's of the 356th Fighter Group in England in 1944. The P-51D's nearest the camera sit in sandbagged revetments. Luftwaffe attacks on bases in England were, by this time, non-existent, making the revetments unnecessary. (Little Friends)

A 5th Emergency Air Sea Rescue Squadron P-47D. The double "W" on the tail denotes "War Weary" and no longer suitable for combat. These aircraft were used to help aircrew that had ditched in the waters around England. Each P-47D was equipped with two droppable life rafts and smoke markers to aid surface craft in locating the downed airmen. (Little Friends)

This 55th Fighter Squadron P-38J 42-104239 KI-P suffered a forced landing on 12 June 1944. The new improved J model, introduced in August 1943, had chin radiators, a flat bulletproof windscreen, power-boosted ailerons and increased fuel capacity. The J model had a top speed of 420 mph at 26,500 feet. (Little Friends)

Gun camera footage from a P-51B flown by Lieutenant-Colonel Glenn Duncan of the 353rd Fighter Group caught this Fw 190 on 22 February 1944. The aircraft crashed shortly after being hit. The 353rd was initially equipped with the P-47 Thunderbolt, converting to the P-51D in October 1944. (NARA)

For many would-be fighter pilots, their first introduction to a high-performance single-seat fighter was the P-39 Airacobra. The P-39N 42-8873 seen here at Oroville, California, during training belonged to the 363rd Fighter Squadron, 357th Fighter Group. (Little Friends)

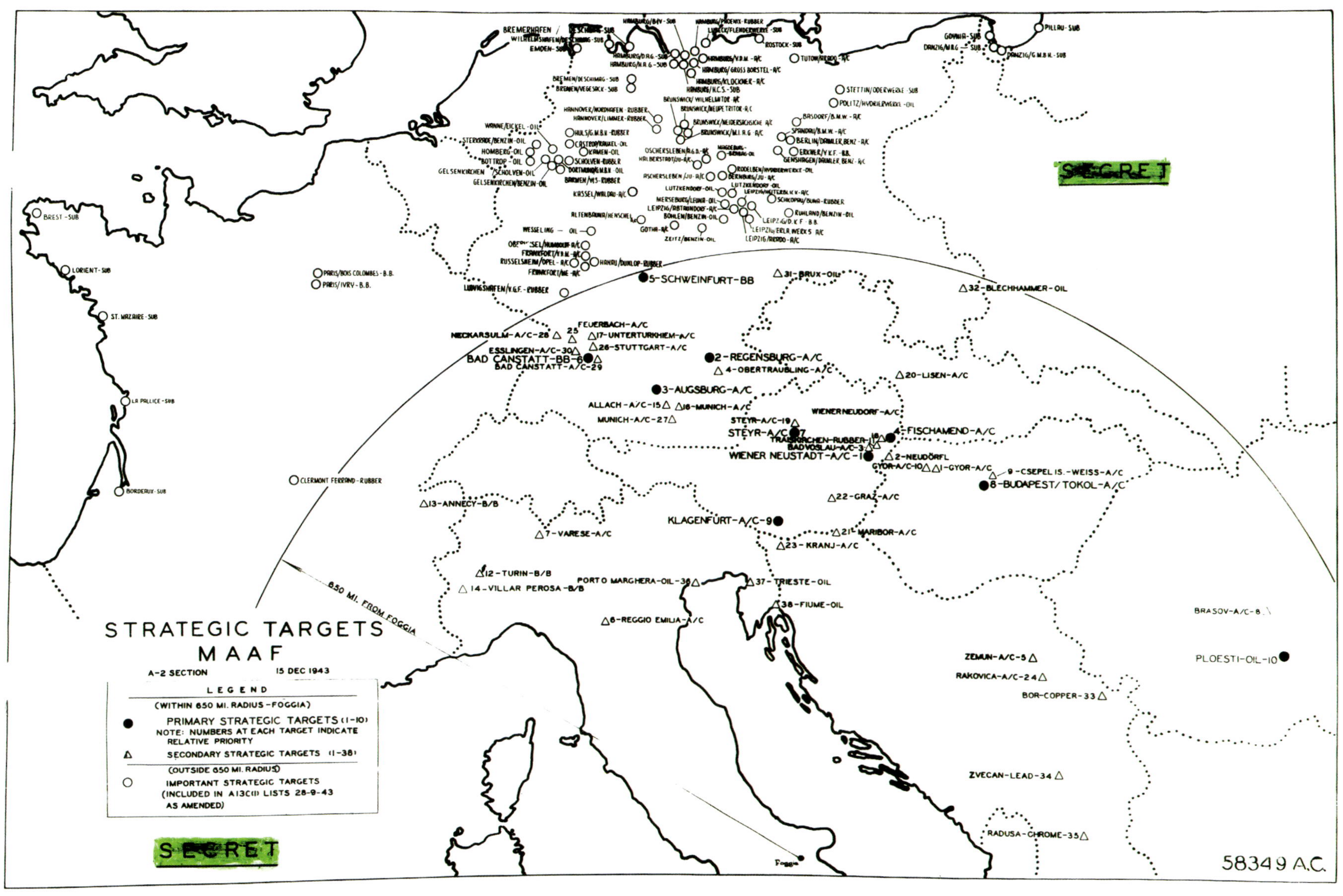

This “Secret” Strategic Targets Mediterranean Army Air Force map shows the combat radius of its heavy bombers from their base at Foggia, Italy. Also noted are the primary strategic targets, secondary targets and other important strategic targets. (NARA)

One of the Allies' primary strategic targets were the oil fields at Ploesti, Romania. This famous photo shows B-24's of the 15th Air Force hitting the Concordia Vega Oil refinery at Ploesti on 31 March 1944. During the war the U.S. Army Air Force mounted 5,287 sorties against this target, with the Royal Air Force contributing 900 night sorties. (NARA)

The North American A-36 was the dive-bomber version of the famous P-51A Mustang. Just 500 were built. They served in North Africa, Sicily and Italy and equipped the 27th and 86th Bombardment Groups of the 12th Air Force. Armed with two 500-pound bombs, the A-36 proved to be an extremely effective ground attack aircraft. (NARA)

In the summer of 1943, the U.S. Army Air Force received more than 100 "reverse Lend-Lease" British Bristol Beaufighter Mk VI night fighters. These aircraft were assigned to the 414th, 415th, 416th and 417th Night Fighter Squadrons based in North Africa and Italy. (NARA)

“Frangible bullets, a new kind of bullet that crumbles on impact, is greatly improving the accuracy of a AAF flexible gunner trainees.” Here a gunnery student in a B-26 top turret shoots at an attacking P-63 Kingcobra using frangible bullets. For use as a target, the P-63 was modified by removing all armament and replacing much of the forward aluminum panels with thicker plate and installing armored glass in the windscreen and side windows. (NARA)

Two North American B-25's churn the water with hits and near misses on a Japanese frigate on 29 March 1945 in the South China Sea. Empty .50-caliber shell casings can be seen being ejected top left from the preceding B-25's attack. In 1943 the U.S. 5th Air Force, based in New Guinea, developed a new type of low-level attack called skip bombing. Modified B-25s were equipped with up to eight nose-mounted .50-caliber machine guns. Flying at mast-top height, the forward-firing guns were used to supress Japanese ship-mounted anti-aircraft guns before the aircraft released their 500-pound bombs. The method proved extremely effective when between 2 and 5 March 1943, B-25s and Australian Beaufighters sank eight Japanese transports and four escorting destroyers in the Bismarck Sea. (NARA)

B-25's of the 12th Bomb Group unload their bombs on Myitkyina airfield in Burma on 23 July 1944. This mission was in support of ground forces trying to reopen the Burma Road to China by retaking the critical airfield. The B-25 was arguably the best medium bomber of the war. The B-25J model was one of the most heavily armed, with 12 nose-mounted 50-caliber machine guns along with 6 guns in the top, waist and tail turrets. It could carry 3,000 pounds of bombs internally. (Author's Collection)

A-20 Havocs proved particularly good at hitting small targets and Japanese coastal shipping. In this photograph A-20's from 3rd Bomb Group have just released their bombs on Japanese lighters in Humbolt Bay, New Guinea. During the war 7,385 A-20s were built, with 3,125 delivered to the Soviet Air Forces. (NARA)

These 14th Air Force P-40 Warhawks were operating in China on 10 August 1944. On 10 March 1943, the Chinese Air Task Force (CATF) was abolished and replaced with the U.S. 14th Air Force, which had 103 P-40's on strength. (NARA)

This 9th Squadron P-38 "Elsie" tail number 88 was damaged during a forced landing at Horanda Airfield, New Guinea, on 5 April 1943. The P-38 was a great success in the Pacific and in the China, Burma and India (CBI) theater of operations. Over 1,800 Japanese aircraft were shot down by P-38's in the Pacific and Asia. (NARA)

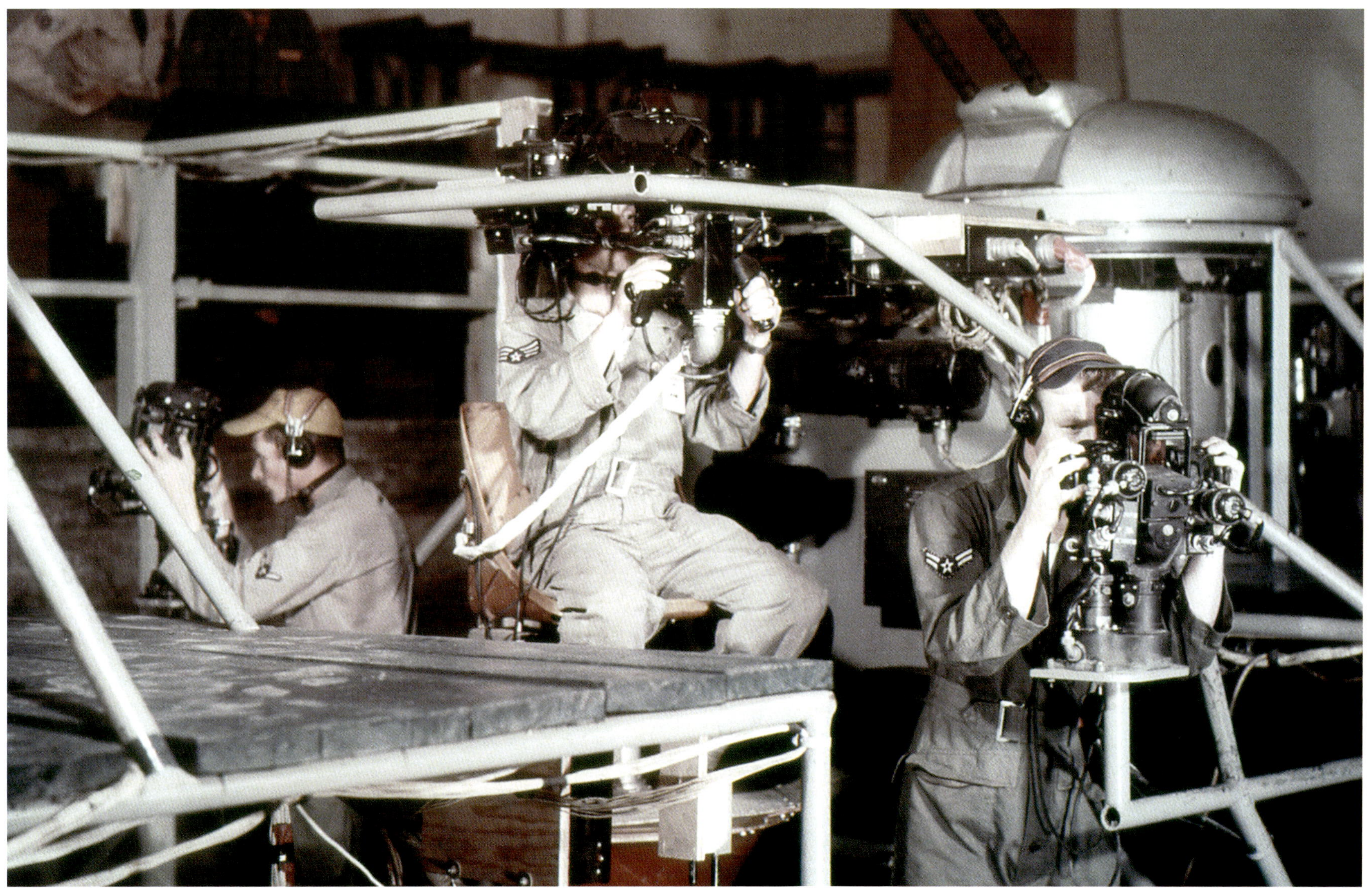

B-29 gunners training in a General Electric fire control simulator. The B-29 was equipped with the world's most advanced analog-computer-aided remote-control fire control system. The B-29 was armed with 12 50-caliber machines guns in four remote-controlled turrets and had a gunner in the tail. (NARA)

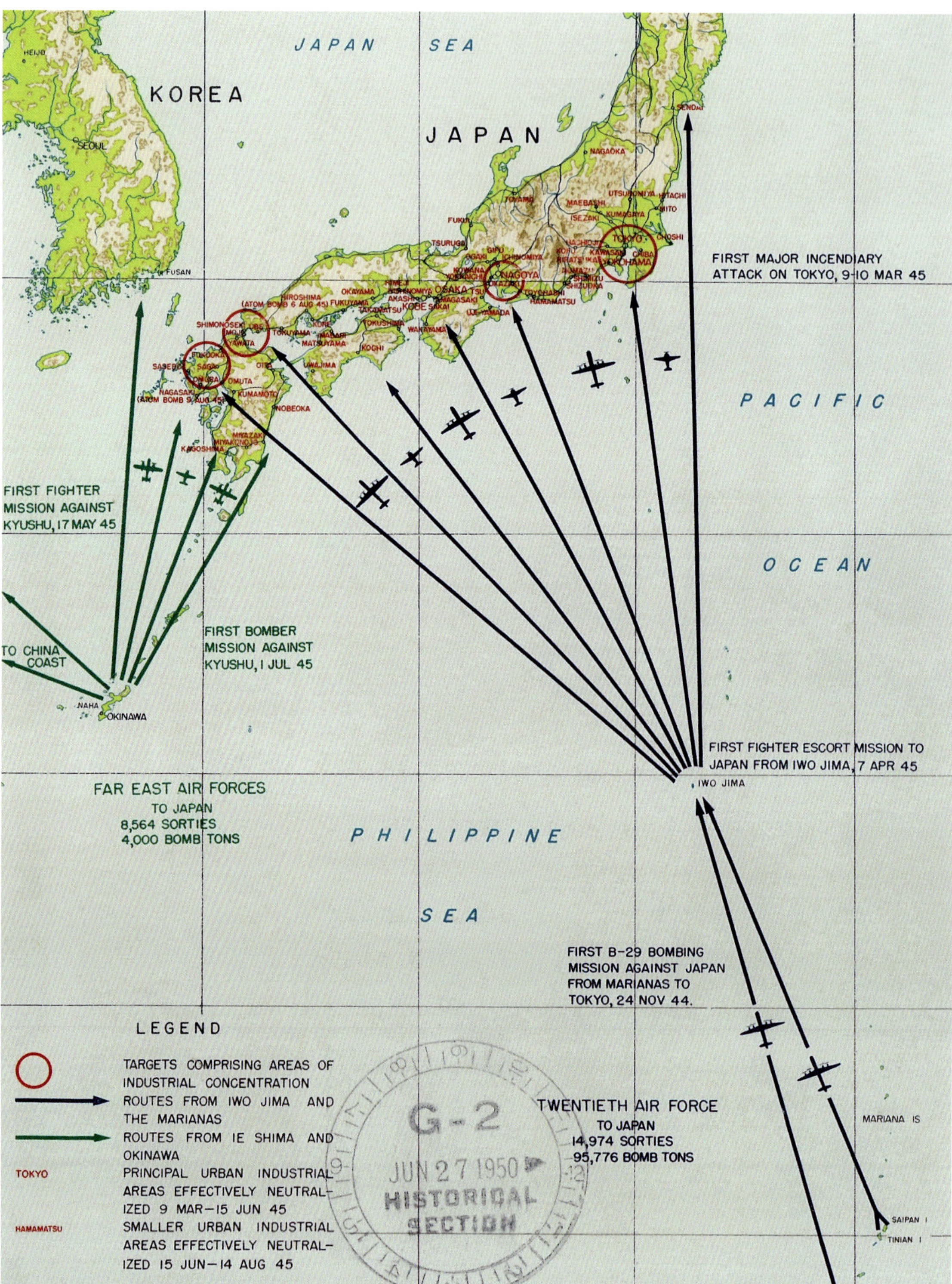

This map shows the power and reach of both the 20th Air Force and Far East Air Forces in 1944–1945. Not only were targets in Japan subject to U.S. Navy carrier-based aircraft attack, but U.S. Army Air Force aircraft from Okinawa, Iwo Jima and the Marinas could hit Japan both day and night at will. (NARA)

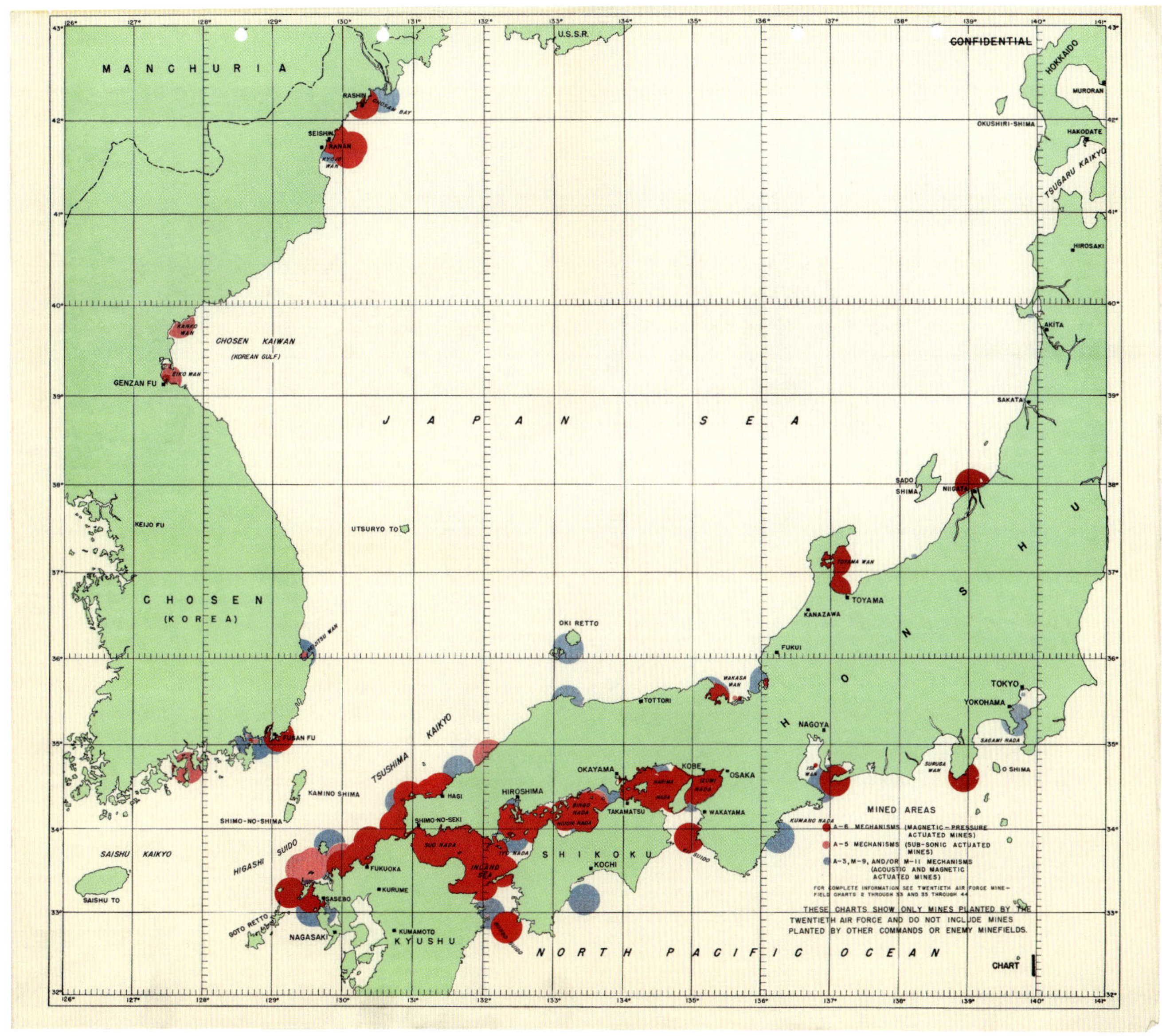

This map shows all the areas around Japan and Korea sown with aerial anti-shipping mines laid by 20th Air Force B-29's. Laying these mines was one of the most successful anti-shipping campaigns of the war and virtually closed off all of Japan's major and minor ports to merchant traffic. Mines laid by B-29's and U.S. Navy submarines sank about 500 merchant and naval vessels. (NARA)

This B-29 "Z-53" 42-65296 of the 883rd Bomb Squadron, 500th Bomb Group is unloading seven 2,000-pound demolition bombs. The AN-M66 General Purpose bomb was almost always used against reinforced structures. The 42-65296 flew 54 missions and survived the war. (Author's Collection)

Consolidated Catalina PBY's being repainted from peace time colors to wartime camouflage. The Catalina was one of the truly great combat aircraft of the war. It was used in many different roles, including anti-submarine, torpedo bomber, air-sea rescue and transport. A total of 3,290 PBY's were built, with 230 coming from Canada. (NARA)

Douglas SBD Dauntless and Grumman TBF Avengers ready for takeoff from an escort carrier on training duty in mid-1943. The SBD proved to be the most successful dive-bomber of the war, sinking, in whole or in part, 6 aircraft carriers, 1 battleship, 3 cruisers, 4 destroyers, 1 submarine and 14 transport ships. (USNHHC)

The F4F-4 Wildcat was introduced into the U.S. Pacific Fleet in April 1942. New features included folding wings, six machine guns, factory-installed armor and self-sealing fuel tanks. (Author's Collection)

The Grumman F6F-3 Hellcat, as seen here in the tricolor camouflage pattern, proved to be the finest carrier-based fighter of the war. From 5 October 1943, when the Hellcat was first introduced, until the end of 1944, Hellcat pilots shot down approximately 1,540 Zero-Sen fighters and 877 Japanese bombers against a loss of 190 Hellcats. Grumman rolled out 12,275 Hellcats during the war. (Author's Collection)

The Vought Chance F4U-1 Corsair was one of the most distinctive fighters of the war. Easily recognized with its long nose and gull wing, the F4U could outperform all the variants of the Mitsubishi Zero-sen in every aspect except slow-speed maneuverability. (NARA)

A Goodyear-built FG-1D of VBF-82 prepares to take off from the carrier USS *Randolph*. The FG-1D had a top speed of 417 mph at 19,000 feet with a range of 1,015 miles. Rate of climb was 2,890 feet per minute at military power. (USNHHC)

FM-2 Wildcats prepare for takeoff from USS *Kitkun Bay* during the battle off Samar in the Philippines on 25 October 1944. In the background, shells from the Japanese battleship *Yamato* can be seen splashing near the escort carrier *White Plains*. During the battle, the six escort carriers of Task Force 3 were caught by a force of four Japanese battleships, six heavy cruisers and small escorts, but just one escort carrier, the *Gambier Bay*, was sunk by Japanese gunfire. (NARA)

The U.S. Navy proved to be an unstoppable force beginning in late 1943. Centered on the Fast Carrier Task Force, it was a combined-arms weapon system that consisted of modern fleet, light and escort carriers along with battleships, cruisers, destroyers, submarines and fleet tankers. (NARA)

A fully loaded Douglas SBD-3 Dauntless dive-bomber carrying one 500-pound and two 100-pound bombs heads out to attack the Japanese base at Truck in April 1944. This aircraft was assigned to VB-18 aboard the carrier USS *Enterprise*. (NARA)

By early 1944 American Essex-class carriers carried 103 aircraft: 73 fighters (Hellcats and Corsairs), 15 Helldiver dive-bombers and 15 Avenger torpedo bombers. Here the USS *Hornet* and *Bonne Homme Richard* turn into the wind in preparation for a strike launch in June 1945. From January 1944 to January 1945, U.S. Navy SBD Dauntless's, SB2Cs Heldivers and TBM Avengers dropped a total of 18,699 tons of bombs on Japanese targets, sinking more than 100 Japanese warships and 200 merchant vessels. (USNHHC)

U.S. Navy carrier-based aircraft attack the Japanese battleship *Haruna* at her moorings near Kure, Japan, on 28 July 1945. During the entire war the U.S. Navy lost just 82 carrier-based dive and torpedo bombers in aerial combat during 60,420 sorties, for loss rate of 0.14 percent. (NARA)

A Reggaine Re 2002 of the 5 Squadron. On 8 September 1943, the Italian Co-Belligerent Air Force had 24 Re 2002's on hand. The Re 2002 was intended to fulfil the fighter bomber role and was capable of carrying 1,433 pounds of bombs. Armament consisted of two 12.7 mm and two 7.7 mm Breda-SAFAT machine guns. The Re 2002's flew their last mission on 2 June 1944. (Author's Collection)

ITALY

Italian Air Force, Italian Co-Belligerent Air Force

On 13 October 1943 the Italian government in southern Italy declared war on Germany and was granted Co-Belligerent status. At the time, these units were located in the south of the country and the air force faced a serious shortage of aircraft, parts, replacement pilots and suitable accommodation. Cut off from Italy's aviation industry in the north, the task of forming a small, efficient air force was a challenging one. It was made even more difficult after the Allies requisitioned the few serviceable airfields and aviation-related overhaul and repair facilities for their own use.

After scouring airfields far and wide, the Italian Co-Belligerent Air Force was able to bring into service a good number of MC.202 fighters and CANT Z.1007 bombers. When serviceability rates began to have a serious effect on operations, the Allies began to supply the Italians with Martin Baltimore bombers and Bell P-39 and Supermarine Spitfire Mk V fighters. Prohibited from operating over Italian territory, the Mediterranean Allied Air Forces deployed the Co-Belligerent squadrons to operate from airfields in the newly liberated areas of the Balkans. These units flew support missions for the Yugoslav partisans fighting the Germans.

By December 1944 the Co-Belligerent Air Force had five groups of fighters equipped with P-39's, Spitfire V's, MC.202's, MC.205's and three squadrons of 36 aircraft each, a mix of Baltimore, S.79, S.82 and Z.1007 bombers.

Combat Aircraft Available September 1943

ITALY CO-BELLIGERENT AIR FORCE, SOUTHERN ITALY/SARDINA

Fighters: 141

Bombers: 16

ITALY

While the American P-39Q replaced the well-worn Macchi MC.205V's in Co-Belligerent Air Force service, the Macchi was the superior fighter and one of the better designs of the war. At the end of the war, the Italians had 60 operational P-39Q's. (Author Collection)

By December 1944, 15th Squadron of 20 Group of the Italian Co-Belligerent Air Force were equipped with Spitfire Mk V's. Later, these aircraft were replaced by newer Mk IX's. (Author's Collection)

The 1 Squadron of the Italian Co-Belligerent Air Force received several well-used ex-Royal Air Force Baltimore IV's and V's in July 1944. As part of the Royal Air Force's Balkan Air Force, the 1 Squadron flew operations over Yugoslavia. (Author's Collection)

A lineup of MC.205V's of the 4th Squadron undergoing engine maintenance in June 1944. Lack of spare parts for the aircraft led the unit to be equipped with Bell P-39Q Airacobra's from U.S. Army Air Force stocks. (Author's Collection)

In Co-Belligerent service, the small number of CANT Z.1007 medium bombers were assigned the task of flying supplies to the Yugoslavian partisans. The Z.1007 operated continuously from 1943 until the end of hostilities. (Author's Collection)

The Savoia Marchetti SM.79bis served in both the Italian Co-Belligerent Air Force in the south and the Italian Republican Air Force in the north. With the Republican Air Force it functioned as a torpedo bomber, and with the Co-Belligerent Air Force it was used as a transport aircraft. During the war the SM.79 was one of the most successful land-based torpedo bombers. It is estimated that SM.79's sank as much as 320,000 tons of allied shipping. (Author's Collection)

The Axis Air Forces

Wrecked Lufwaffe aircraft litter the Waalhaven airfield shortly after the surrender of the Dutch Armed Forces. The wrecks include a Ju 52 transport, a Do 17 and a Henschel Hs 126. (AAM)

GERMANY

German Air Force

When the new Luftwaffe came into existence in 1935, Germany had the advantage of a first-class aircraft industry with excellent designers and engineers, a huge, modern industrial base and a highly trained workforce. Having been prohibited from producing military aircraft under the terms of the 1919 Treaty of Versailles, the Germans were not encumbered by the old metal and fabric methods of construction.

Having gained experience in the late 1920s and 1930s, German aviation began building a series of ever more advanced mail planes, airliners and touring and sports aircraft. Many advanced aviation design techniques were tested and incorporated into these new aircraft, including low-set cantilever wings, stressed-skin semi-monocoque fuselage shells, retractable landing gear, radios and enclosed cockpits. Soon manufacturers like Heinkel, Arado, Dornier, Focke-Wulf, Junkers and, of course, Messerschmitt were building some of the most feared aircraft of World War II.

One example was the famous Messerschmitt Bf 109, whose design began in secret in March 1934. When the Bf 109 V1 prototype emerged for its first flight on 28 May 1935, it was arguably the most advanced design in the world. New modern aircraft would follow, including bombers like the Heinkel He 111, Dornier Do 17, Junkers Ju 88, Junkers Ju 87 and Messerschmitt Me 110 long-range fighter. However, the Nazis had not envisioned a long war in Europe and devoted just one-sixth of the economy to military production. As a result, Luftwaffe strength at the beginning of war was 3,960 aircraft of all types. While the numbers were impressive, production rates remained dangerously low, and by 1940 both Britain and Canada were manufacturing more aircraft than Germany.

The Luftwaffe accepted foreign nationals into it ranks, but reluctantly. Due to basic ideological reservations and prejudices, Hitler and other leading Nazis viewed foreign nationals with suspicion. By 1943 that view had changed, and airmen from Alsace-Lorraine, Spain, Italy, Russia, Croatia, Norway, Estonia, Latvia, Netherlands and Belgium joined the ranks of the Luftwaffe. These were not all volunteers, however, with many given the stark choice of service in the Waffen SS or Luftwaffe.

Combat Aircraft Available September 1939

Fighters: 1,174

Bombers: 1,180

Dive-Bombers: 366

Ground Attack: 40

Maritime/Patrol: 240

Reconnaissance: 604

GERMANY

A German ground crew takes a break in front of Bf 109E-1 of III./JG 53 in the autumn of 1939. The period from October 1939 to May 1940 was known as the "Phoney War," but in reality the skies along the western front were marked by an escalating series of small but bitterly fought engagements. Bf 109's were credited with 160 kills during this period, with 73 credited to the JG 53. (Author's Collection)

This Bf 109E-3, belonging to I/JG 76, was captured on 22 November 1939 and subsequently fell into French hands. It was shipped to the United States in April 1942 for trials and testing. Compared to the clean lines of the Spitfire, the Bf 109 was more angular and business-like in appearance. (NASM)

These Junkers Ju 87 Stukas are being prepared for another mission during the invasion of Poland in September 1939. The Ju 87 is credited with the first Luftwaffe air-to-air kill, when a Stuka from I./StG 2 shot down an unsuspecting Polish PZL fighter from behind on 1 September 1939. (Author's Collection)

This rare photo shows a Heinkel He 111 flying in formation with a Heinkel He 100 fighter. The He 100 was not adopted for Luftwaffe service, but the examples built were used for a series of propaganda photographs, and it was dubbed the He 113. (AAM)

Air and ground crew of a Bf 110C-1 service their aircraft in the summer of 1939. The Bf 110 proved a versatile and effective fighter, bomber, night fighter and reconnaissance aircraft. Total of 6,170 Bf 110's were produced during the war. (Author's Collection)

A Do 17Z of I./KG 2 practices a low-level airfield attack. Due to its good handling characteristics, the Dornier bomber was used exclusively in low-level operations during the Polish campaign in September 1939, during the invasion of the Low Countries and France in May 1940 and during the Battle of Britain. (Author's Collection)

A Bf 109E-4/B “Jabo” on the ground in France. The Bf 109E-4/B and Bf 110D-0 fighter bomber from Erprobungsgruppe 210 were arguably the most successful Luftwaffe bombers during the Battle of Britain. These low-level attacks proved a major problem for British defenses. (Author’s Collection)

A Luftwaffe pilot gives a helping hand to his ground crew as they service his Bf 109E-3. The Bf 109E proved to be one of the most effective fighters in the world from 1939 until the beginning of 1941, when it was replaced by the Bf 109F variant. (Author's Collection)

This burning Heinkel He 111H-3 was hit by anti-aircraft fire and finished off by Spitfires on 11 September 1940. The pilot made a forced landing at Broomhill Farm near Camber, England. The He 111 was one of the mainstays of the assault on Britain in 1940–1941 and first saw Luftwaffe service during the Spanish Civil War. (Author's Collection)

A formation of fully loaded Ju 87B's, each carrying a single SC 250 and four SC 50 bombs, of III./StG 51 head out for another daylight raid against British targets. The Stuka and the Bf 109/Bf 110 "Jabos" were the most accurate Luftwaffe bombers that fought during the Battle of Britain. (Author's Collection)

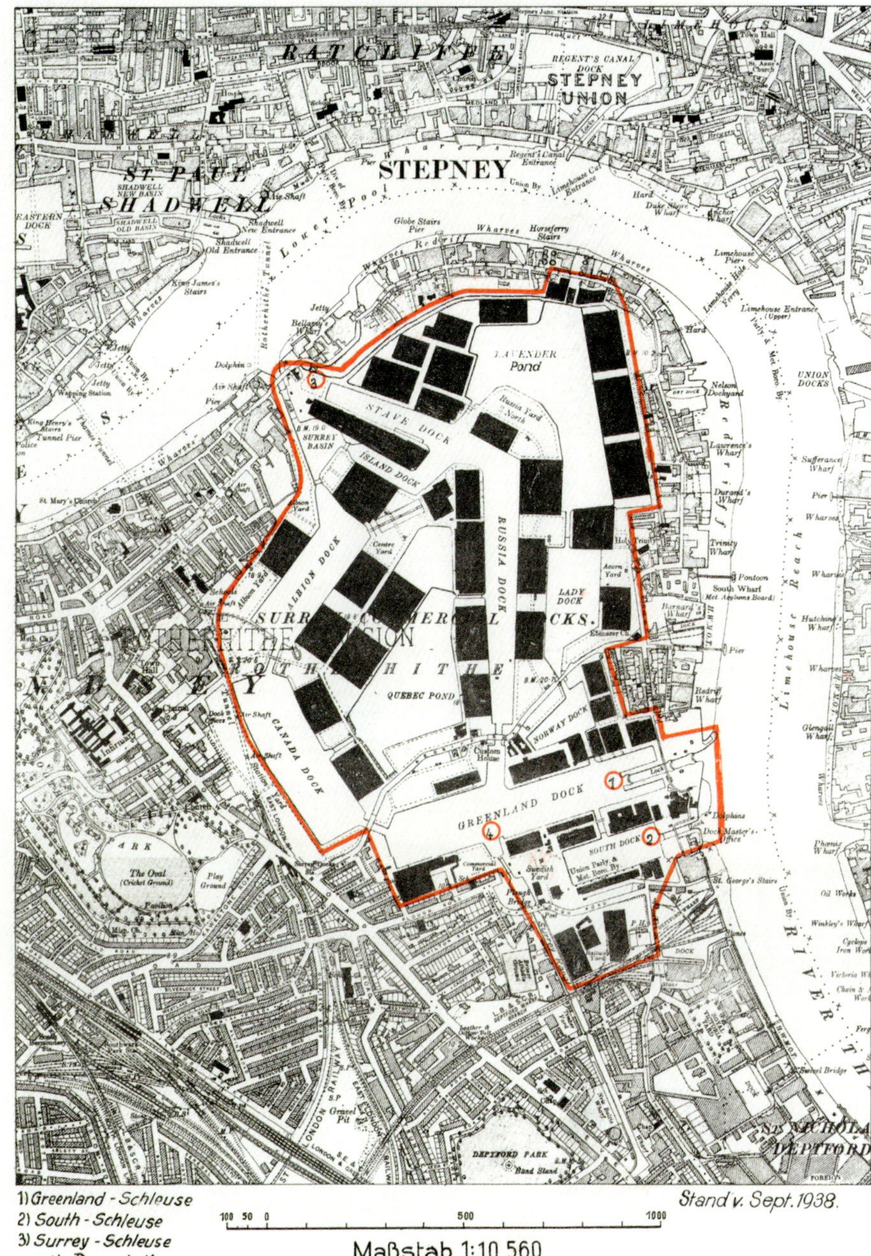

This target map shows the prime dock targets for German bombers. It would have been used by the crew in the aircraft pictured on the opposite page. (Author's Collection)

This is one of the most famous photographs of World War II. It shows a Heinkel He 111 over the London docks, visible behind the starboard wing, on 7 September 1940. (Author's Collection)

This black camouflaged Ju 88A-5 is being loaded with a single SC 1000 (2,000-pound) bomb for a night attack on England late in 1940. The Ju 88 was used extensively during the "Blitz" in 1940–1941, and by the end of September 1940 the Ju 88 equipped four complete Kampfgeschwader with five more units in the process of conversion. (Author's Collection)

It wasn't until after the Battle of Britain that the Bf 109 was equipped with an external fuel tank. It's anemic range of 412 miles on internal fuel put it at a distinct disadvantage during a battle. This pilot readies the aircraft for his next flight in his Bf 109E-7/Trop in Sicily in 1941. (Author's Collection)

This Bf 109G-6 is being prepared for another mission. The G-6 was armed with two 13 mm MG 131 machine guns and a single 20 mm MG 151 machine gun firing through the propeller hub. The G-6 had a top speed of 386 mph at 22,640 feet. A staggering 12,000 Bf 109G-6's were produced between 1942 and June 1944. (Author's Collection)

Bf 110D-0 fighter bombers being prepared for another mission in the early stages of the invasion of Holland, Belgium and France, May 1940. The Bf 110D-0 was equipped with two ETC 550 racks, located just below the pilot's cockpit, and could carry two SC 500 (1,100-pound) bombs. (Author's Collection)

This mixed formation of Bf 109G-5/6's from 7./JG 27 are on a bomber escort mission above the Adriatic Sea in January 1943. The two Bf 109G's in the background are in the 'Kannonenboot' (gunboat) configuration, each armed with two underwing 20 mm cannon gondolas. (Author's Collection)

A factory-fresh Bf 110G-4/R1 night fighter equipped the FuG 212 Lichtenstein C1 radar. The additional radar array and exhaust shrouds around the engines effectively cut the speed of the Bf 110G-4 by 25 mph. With added fuel tanks, the speed would be reduced even more. (AAM)

Armed with four WGR 21 air-to-air rocket propelled mortar shells and two 20 mm and two 30 mm cannons, the Bf 110 was arguably the most heavily armed twin-engine fighter of the war. In the fall of 1943, the Germans began to equip their Bf 110s with the Wfr. G21 aerial rockets to break up American bomber formations. (Author's Collection)

A small number of Bf 110G's were equipped with a single 37 mm Flack 18 automatic cannon to battle U.S. Army Air Force heavy bombers. The weapon's low rate of fire exposed attacking Bf 110 pilots to the concentrated fire from American tail gunners, making the aircraft ineffective in combat. (Author's Collection)

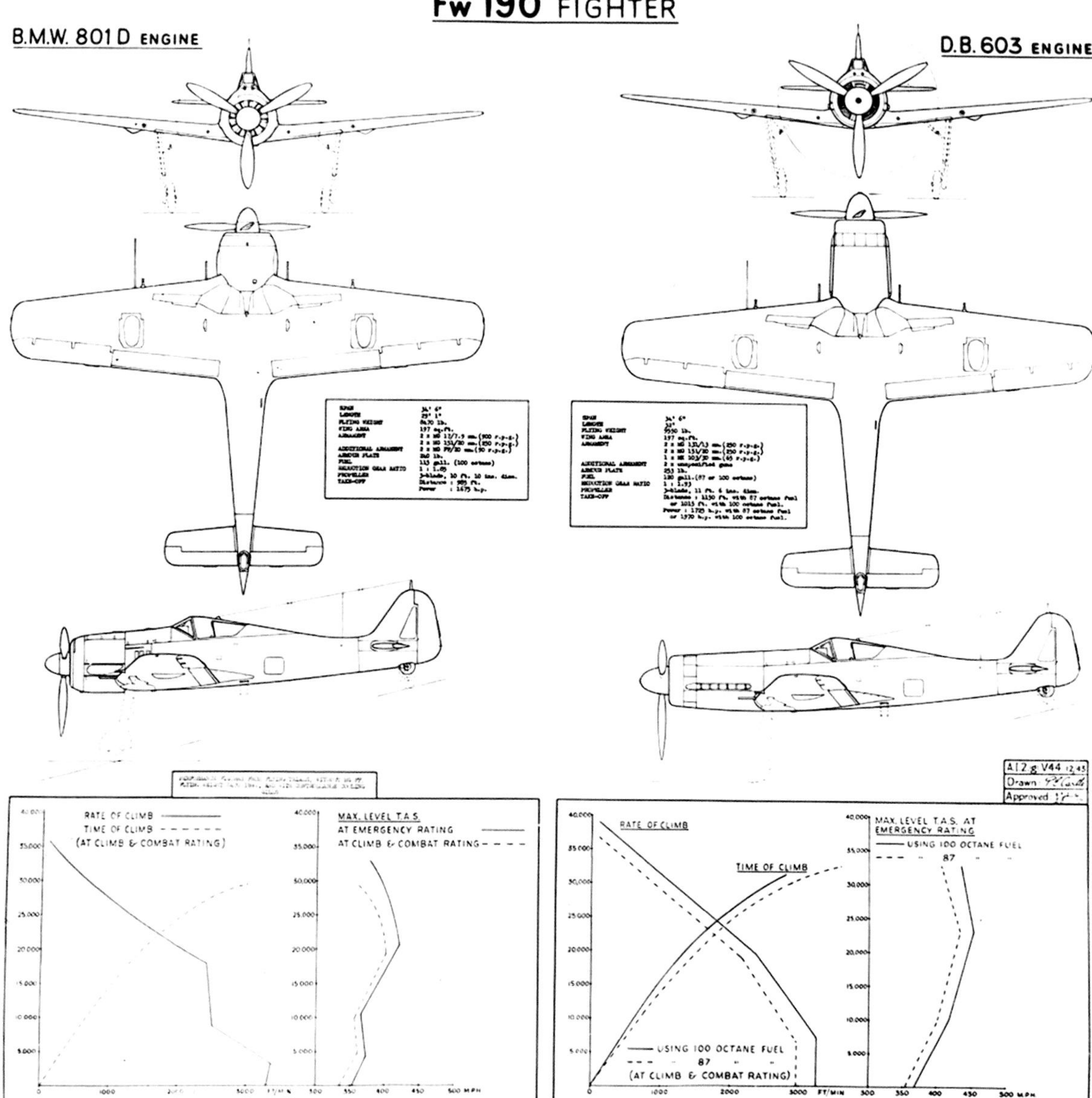

This British Air Intelligence drawing shows the performance differences between the radial engine Fw 190A and the new inline engine Fw 190D. To address the Fw 190A's poor high-altitude performance, the Fw 190 was redesigned and fitted with the Jumo 213A-1 liquid-cooled engine (not the D.B. 603 as listed on the drawing), producing the Fw 190D-9 Dora-9. The Dora-9 was unquestionably the best piston-engine fighter to see service with the Luftwaffe. (Author's Collection)

The Luftwaffe operated several different float- and seaplanes during the war. The most successful were the Dornier Do 24, Heinkel He 115 and Blohm and Voss BV 138. This Royal Air Force aircraft identification poster provides three angle views for each aircraft. (Author's Collection)

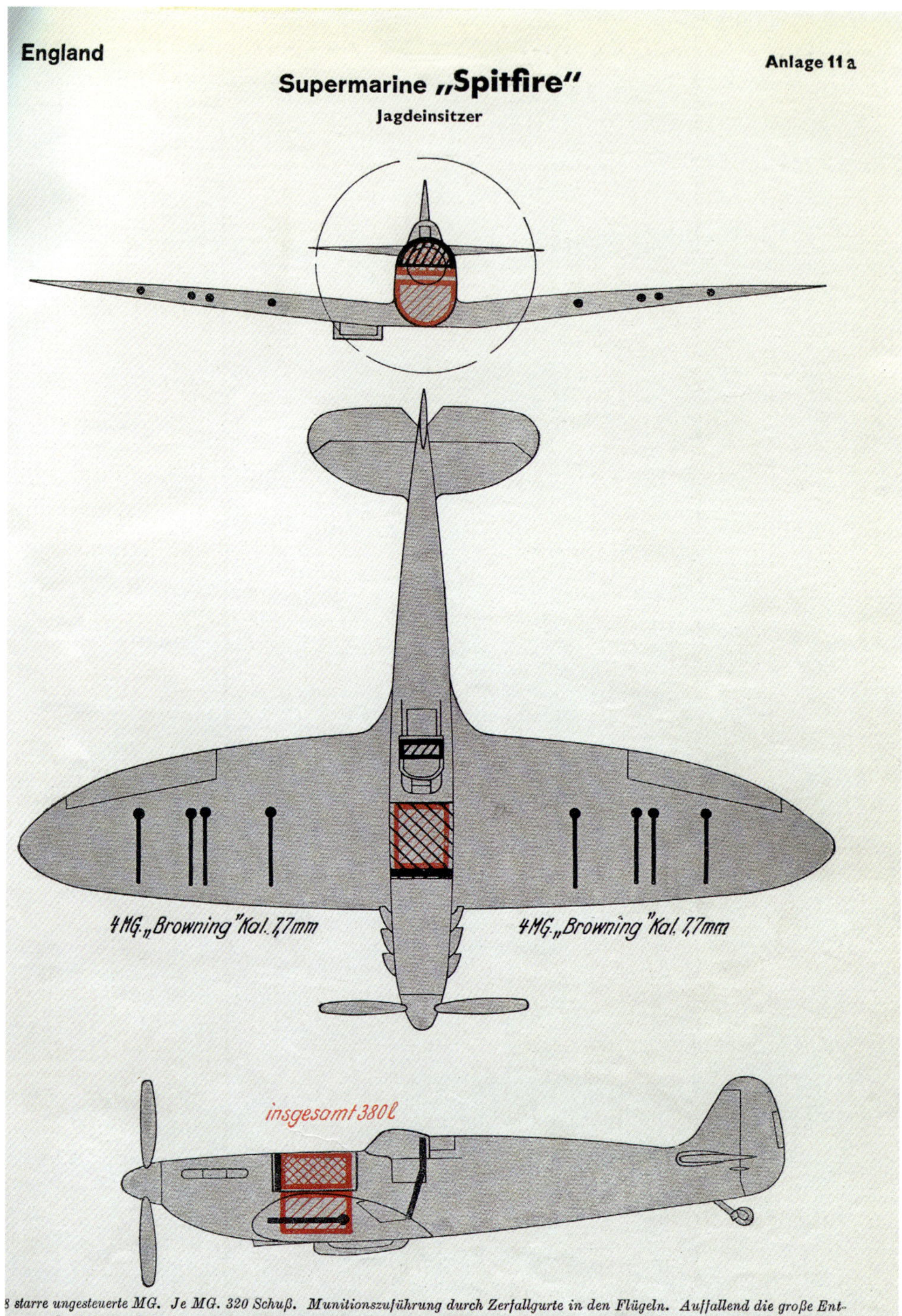

This Luftwaffe identification drawing of the Supermarine Spitfire highlights the aircraft's armament, self-sealing fuel tanks and armor plating. (Author's Collection)

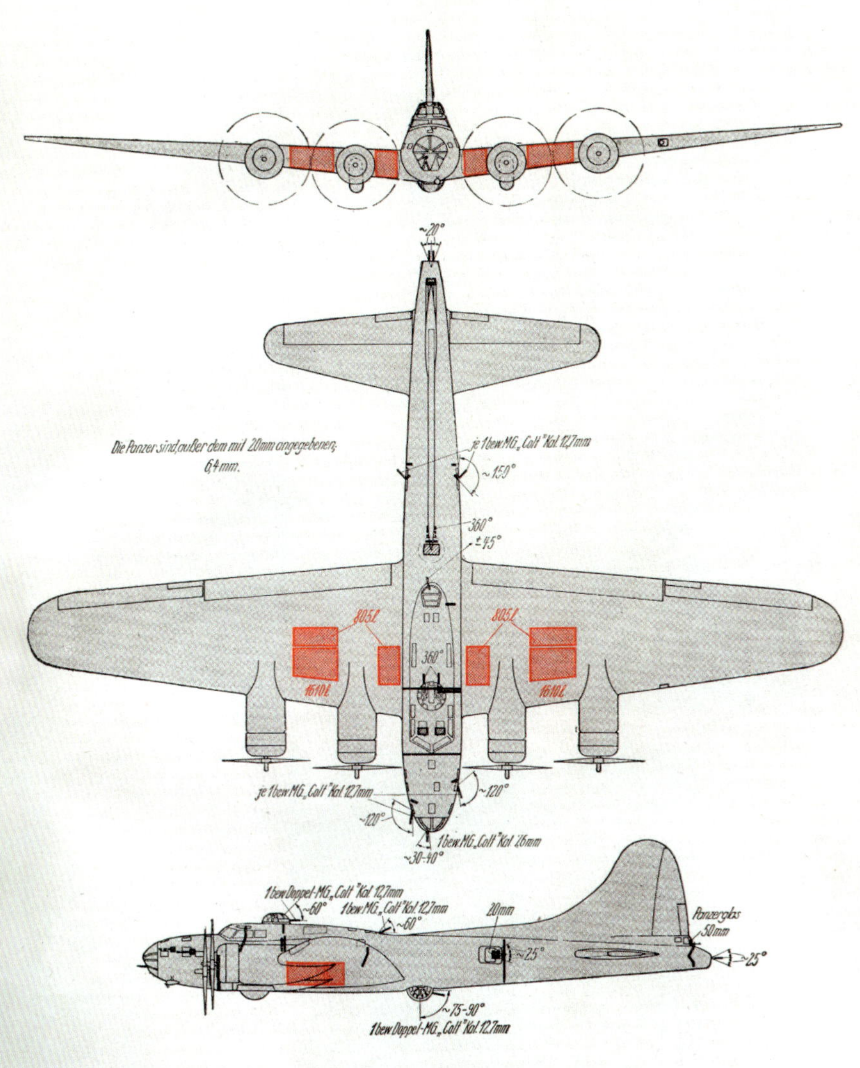

A Luftwaffe identification drawing of the B-17F. This three-view drawing shows the location of the armor plate, self-sealing fuel tanks, armament and firing angles for each gun. To shoot down a B-17 required considerable pilot skill. Attacking a Flying Fortress from either the side or behind would attract determined return fire from the various gun positions. A Bf 109 or Fw 190 pilot would have to be very skillful and determined in order to achieve a victory against a B-17. (Author's Collection)

This is one of the first British Air Intelligence cutaway drawings of a Do 217E Luftwaffe bomber. The Dornier Do 217E did not enter service until late 1940 and was the first model of the Do 217's capable of carrying a bombload of 8,818 pounds. Some 1,541 Do 217's were built, with another 364 Do 217N-2's produced as night fighters. (Author's Collection)

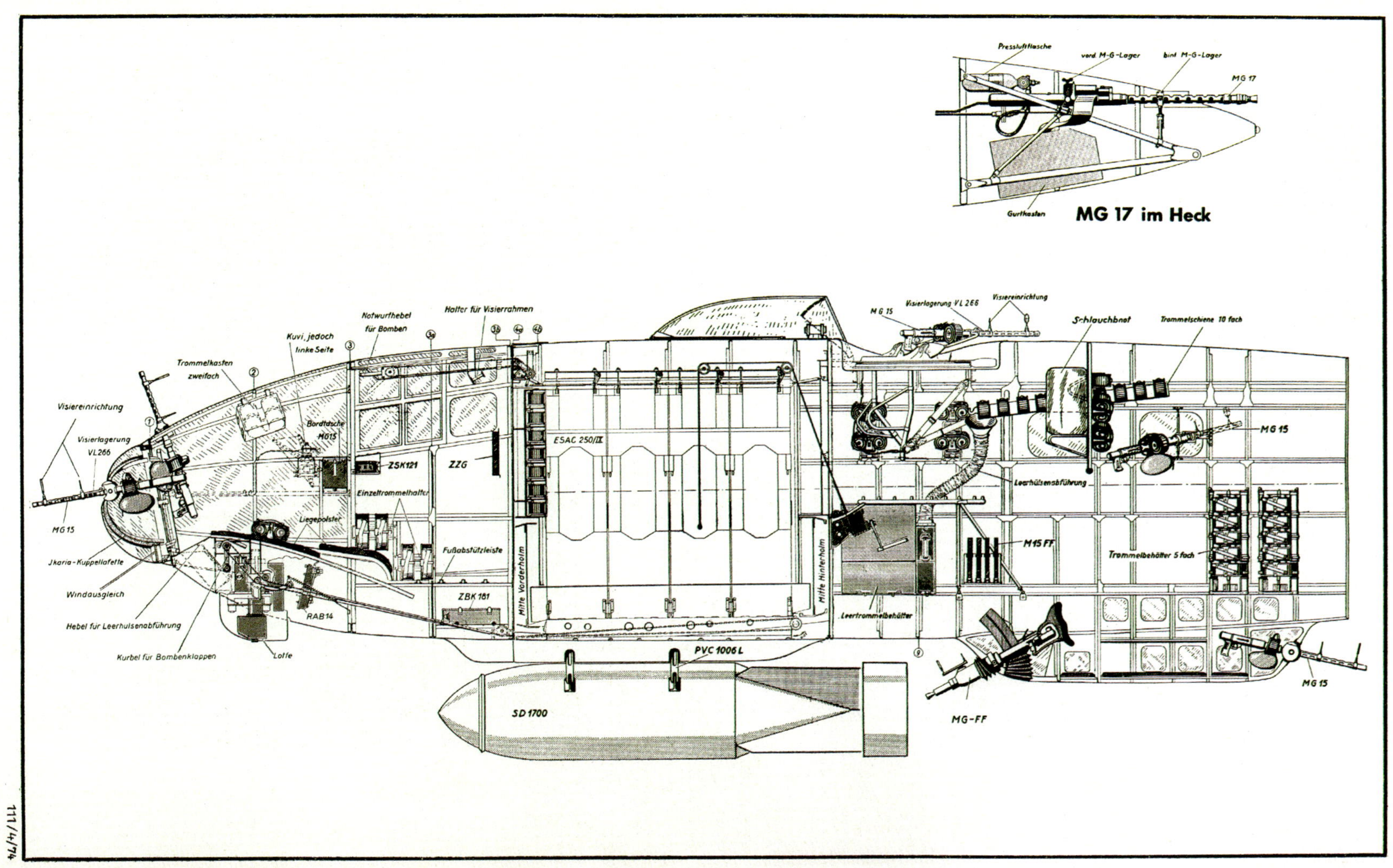

Abb. 28: Gesamtübersicht der Bewaffnung He 111 H-5

This 1940–1941armament drawing shows the He 111H-5. The He 111H-5 was the most widely used Luftwaffe bomber during the "Blitz" over England. With external bomb racks, the He 111H-5 could carry two 2,205-pound bombs. (Author's Collection)

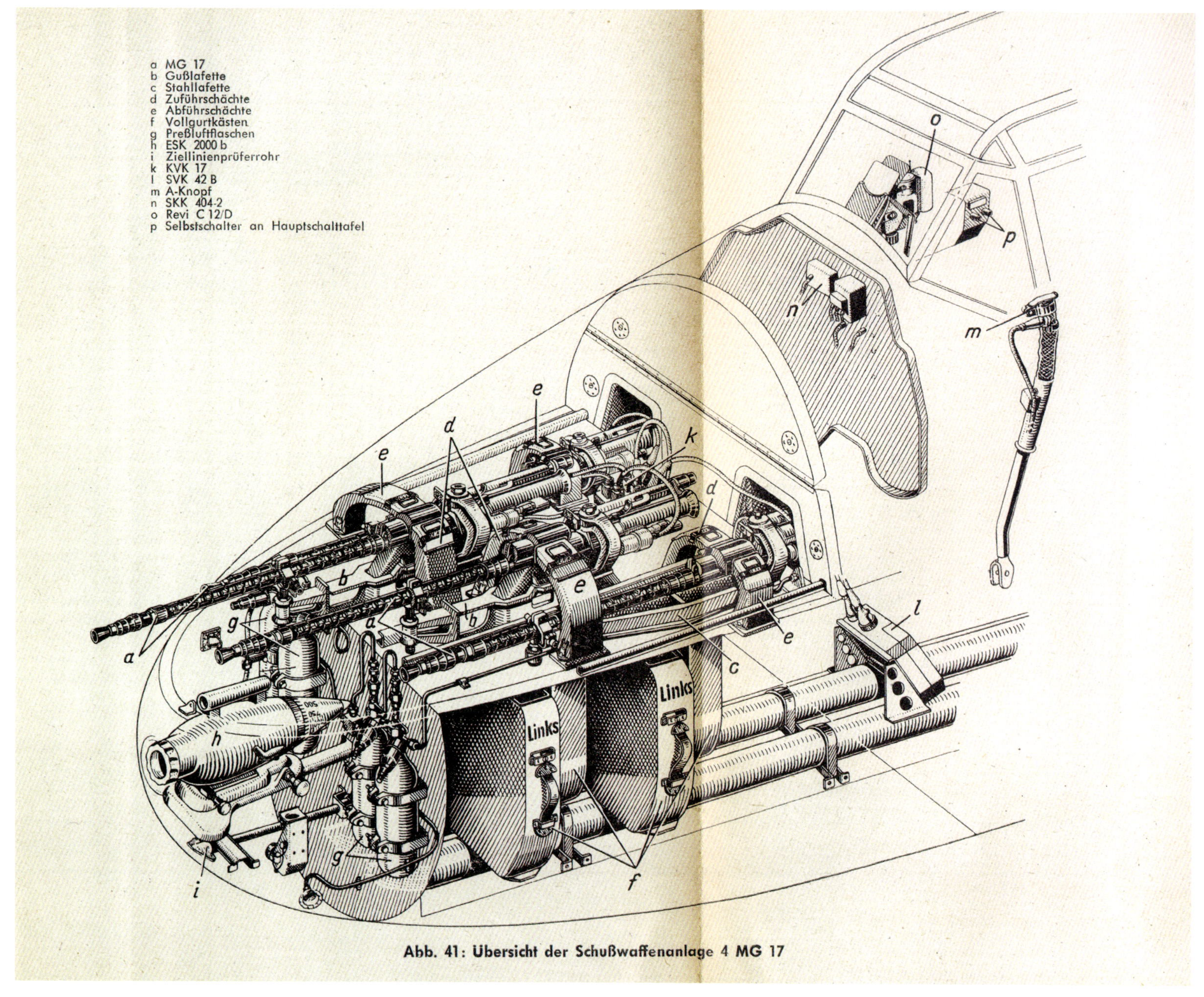

The Messerschmitt Me 110 was well-armed with four 7.92 mm MG 17 and two 20 mm MG 151 cannons. The blast tubes for the 20 mm cannon can be seen underneath the ammunition magazines. (Author's Collection)

A stepped-up formation of Do 17Z's on 15 September 1940. Despite being the least capable of the Luftwaffe's medium bombers, it was used widely during the Battle of Britain. This was the Luftwaffe's last mass daylight attack on London. The Do 17Z carried five flexibly mounted 7.92 mm MG 15 machine guns. These were drum fed, with each drum holding 75 rounds. Spare magazines were held on special brackets arranged near each gun. (Author's Collection)

Two Me 262A-1's taxi out for a training mission at Lechfeld airfield in Bavaria. These belong to III/EJG 2, the official training establishment for all future Me 262 fighter pilots. Adolf Galland, Inspector of Fighters, was of the opinion that if the Luftwaffe had "300 Me 262 jet fighters we could have on any given day shot down a minimum of 200 bombers." (Author's Collection)

The Ju 188E-2 torpedo bomber was equipped with air to surface FuG 200 Hohenweil radar. The aircraft could carry two 1,763-pound torpedoes. During the war, Luftwaffe torpedo bomber units sank 68 merchant ships and 6 Allied warships. (Author's Collection)

A captured Blohm & Voss BV 222C-012 Wiking flying boat seen here at Trondheim, Norway, in 1945. This version was powered by six Jumo 207c diesel engines. The BV 222 was used both in a maritime patrol and transport role. Just seven examples of this aircraft survived the war. (NARA)

This Focke Wulf Fw 200C-8/U10 is armed with a pair of Henschel Hs 293A anti-shipping missiles. The missile-carrying Fw 200 was not a success, but beginning in mid-1943, Hs 293 missiles (launched from He 111's and Do 217's) sank several Allied ships, mostly in the Mediterranean theater. (Author's Collection)

A Blohm & Voss BV 138 and a Heinkel He 115 at Kirkenes in Norway in 1943. Both aircraft served in maritime patrol, anti-shipping, anti-submarine, mine, laying and U-boat reconnaissance roles. The BV 138C-1 was armed with one 20 mm MG 151 cannon, one 13 mm MG 131 machine gun and one 7.92 mm MG 15 machine gun. Bombload was up to six 110-pound bombs or four 331-pound depth charges. The He 115B-1 was armed with one forward-firing and one rear-firing 7.92 mm MG 15 machine gun and carried a maximum bombload of 2,760 pounds. (Author's Collection)

The Fw 190A-8/R2 Sturmbocke was designed to be a heavy-bomber killer. It had armored cockpit glass, side armor plating for the cockpit and an armament of two 30 mm Mk 108 cannons and two 20 mm MG 151 cannons. The Fw 190A-8/R2 was considered to be the first Fw 190 variant able to hold its own against the massed defensive firepower of U.S. Army Air Force B-17 and B-24 formations and to be sufficiently armed to cause considerable damage to them. (Author's Collection)

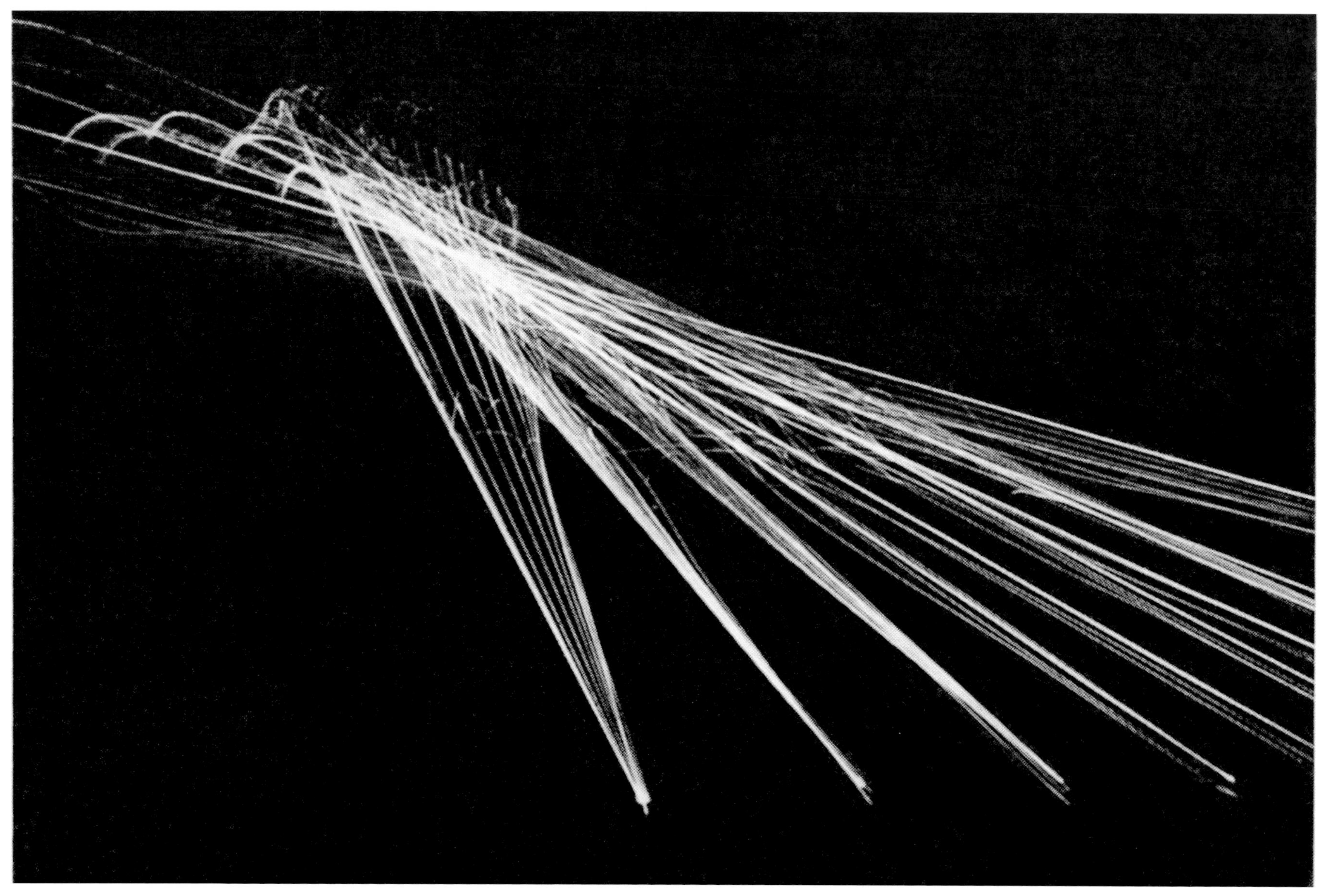

The anti-aircraft defense of Germany was the responsibility of the Luftwaffe. Here, a stream of 37 mm tracer fire concentrate on a single point. The RAF's Short Stirling bomber was vulnerable to light and medium flak such as this due to its low operating ceiling height. A fully loaded Stirling Mk I was hard pressed to reach 12,000 feet. (Author's Collection)

The Junkers Ju 290A-4 maritime patrol bomber of KG 200 in flight. Very few Ju 290's were built, with production totaling about 45 transports. Maritime reconnaissance production added a further 37 aircraft. The Ju 290A-4's defensive armament consisted of five 20 mm MG 151 cannons and one 13 mm MG 131 machine gun. (NARA)

The Bf 109G-6's armament of one 20 mm cannon and two 13 mm machine guns was too light and ineffective against the U.S. Army Air Force B-17 and B-24 bombers. To increase its armament, two underwing 20 mm cannons were added. These aircraft were nicknamed "Gunboats." However, the increased armament reduced overall speed and maneuverability. (Author's Collection)

Captured examples of the Fw 190A-8 and Bf 109G-10/R2. While production of both aircraft increased in 1944, poor quality and reliability proved a major problem. Sabotage by slave laborers left many airframes unfit for combat. (Author's Collection)

Two captured Bf 109G-6/Trops left behind by II./JG53 at Comiso, Sicily. The Bf 109G-6's performance was beginning to fall behind the newer Allied fighters that were being introduced in 1943. Both the P-51B/C Mustang and P-47D Thunderbolt were faster by as much as 60 mph. (Author's Collection)

An Fw 190G-3 fighter bomber at Montecorvino airfield near Salerno, Italy, in 1943. The Fw 190 ground-attack version of this aircraft proved to be extremely effective. The G-3 version with greatly strengthened undercarriage could carry 3,968 pounds of bombs. (Author's Collection)

Two He 177 heavy bombers caught on the ground by marauding Allied fighters. The ground crew can be seen running from their aircraft. The He 177 was a complete failure as a heavy bomber. Engine fires were common, and the problem was never fully solved. (Author's Collection)

An Arado Ar 234B-2 jet bomber being serviced and made ready for another mission. Just a handful of these jets saw service during the war, with the first becoming operational with KG 76 in October 1944. Just 210 Ar 234B-1's and B-2's were built during the last months of the war. (Author's Collection)

The Japanese carrier *Kaga* turns into the wind and readies its aircraft for launch. On deck are Nakajima A2N fighters, Aichi D1A dive-bombers and Mitsubishi B2M torpedo aircraft. Just 24 hours after the outbreak of war between China and Japan in 1937, aircraft from the carriers *Hosho*, *Ryugo* and *Kaga* began striking targets along the Chinese coast. (Author's Collection)

JAPAN

Japanese Army Air Force, Japanese Naval Air Force

Well before the attack on Pearl Harbor on 7 December 1941, the Japanese focused their military budget on the production of aircraft and naval vessels. By the mid-1930s the trajectory of Japanese aircraft design and production began to change, and dependence on foreign technology and assistance began to decrease. Western intelligence estimates of Japanese technology began to slip in quality and quantity. By the mid-1930s, the accepted view was that the Japanese were incapable of extensive technical innovation. The typical Western view was that the Japanese were "notorious copyists."

This view was still strong in the first year of the war, when U.S. Navy pilots reported seeing German Me 109 fighters during the Battle of Midway. But the truth was that the Japanese were modifying foreign designs to suit their own needs rather than simply copying them wholesale. In addition, an increasing number of designs were entirely of Japanese origin. Despite the shortage of machine tools, skilled labor and heavy equipment, the Japanese were making great strides. At the same time, they weren't averse to ordering foreign aircraft. In 1938, they ordered 82 Italian Fiat BR.20 bombers for service in China.

By 1937 several capable and effective combat aircraft entered service in China. One of the first was the monoplane Mitsubishi A5M Type 96 "Claude" naval fighter, followed by the long-range Mitsubishi G3M Type 96 "Nell" bomber, the Nakijima Ki-27 "Nate" monoplane fighter and finally the famous A6M2 Model 21 "Zero" in September 1940. Even when the evidence was clear that the Japanese had achieved technological parity with the West, and superiority in some cases, the Western powers often belittled or ignored the Japanese achievement.

Like the Germans, the Japanese had planned for a short war. A war of attrition in the air with the United States was out of the question for Japan. Their industrial capacity had no hope of matching that of the United States. In December 1941 the Japanese Army and Naval air forces possessed the most powerful and best trained carrier-based attack forces in the world. They also had the largest number of land-based strike aircraft in the Pacific, including approximately 400 A6M2 Model 21 Zero-sen's, of which 108 took part in the attack on Pearl Harbor on 7 December 1941.

Combat Aircraft Available December 1941

JAPANESE NAVAL AIR FORCE

Fighters: 660

Carrier Strike Aircraft: 330

Land-Based Bombers: 240

Seaplanes/Flying Boats: 325

JAPANESE ARMY AIR FORCE

Fighters: 648

Bombers: 940

The Nakajima Ki-27 "Nate" began operations in China in March 1938. The Ki-27 would be the Japanese army's main fighter until the attack on Pearl Harbor. With a maximum speed of 290 mph and an armament of just two 7.7 mm Type 89 machine guns, it was obsolete by December 1941. (Author's Collection)

The design of the Aichi D1A Type 96 dive-bomber was based on the German Heinkel He 50. The D1A code named "Susie" could carry a single 551-pound bomb and two 66-pound bombs. The D1A2 was used in combat in a secondary role until 1942. (NARA)

Sergeant E.L. Sadler, a pilot with No. 67 Squadron, poses with a Japanese Army Nakajima Ki-27 Type 97 fighter that was shot down near Rangoon, Burma. This aircraft, piloted by Captain Fujio Sakaguchi, was downed on 24 January 1942. (RNZAFM)

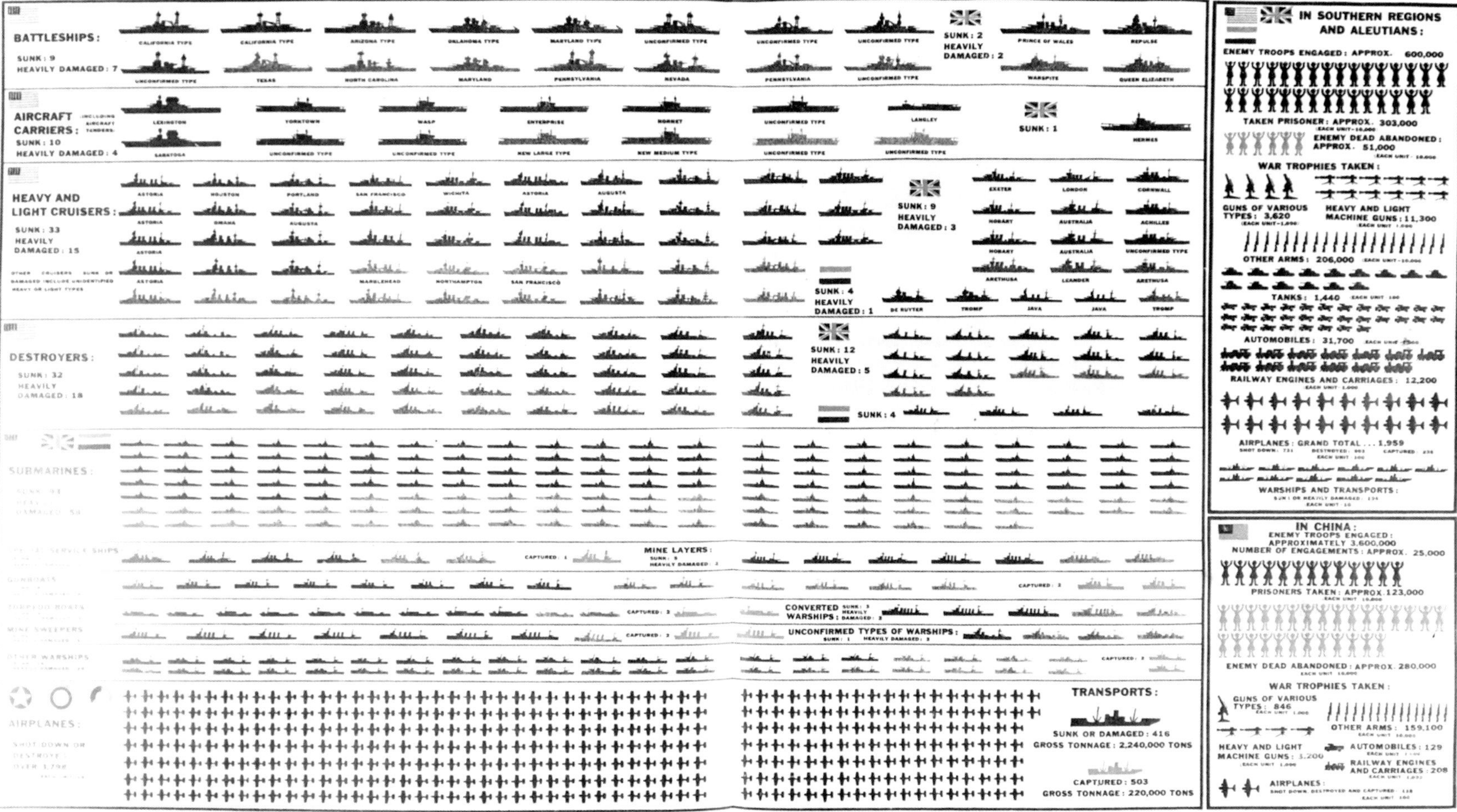

This Japanese propaganda poster boosts of "Brillant Results" during the first year of the war. However, the information presented was pure fantasy. During the first year of combat the U.S. Navy lost four fleet carriers and one light carrier and the Royal Navy lost the carrier *Hermes* to Japanese action, not the 10 listed here. (LOC)

The Mitsubishi A5M4 "Claude" was introduced in 1937. This Japanese Naval Air Force carrier-based fighter was the fastest in the world at the time, with a maximum speed of 270 mph. It was also one of the first fighters to use an external drop tank holding 42 gallons of fuel. It had an impressive range of 750 miles. (Author's Collection)

With the deck crew waving, an A6M2 Zero-sen takes off bound for the attack on Pearl Harbor. The Zero-sen was the Japanese Naval Air Force's premiere fighter and would remain in production until the end of the war, with a total of 10,094 being built. It was the most maneuverable carrier-based fighter of the Pacific campaign thanks to its large wing area and generously proportioned ailerons. (NARA)

A Nakajima B5N2 Type 97 Carrier Attack Plane “Kate” takes off from the carrier *Shokaku* en route to attack Pearl Harbor. During the attack, the “Kate” was used both as a torpedo bomber and horizontal bomber. It was armed with a single armor-piercing bomb. (USNHHC)

Mitsubishi Ki-21 "Sally." The Ki-21 was the Japanese Army's principal bomber during the war in China. Lightly constructed and initially not equipped with self-sealing fuel tanks or armor, it was an easy target for well-armed Allied fighters like the Hawker Hurricane Mk I, Curtiss Hawk 81A and Brewster Buffalo I. (Author's Collection)

These land-based Aichi D3A2 “Vals” are ready for takeoff. From the autumn of 1944, land-based Vals were increasingly used as kamikaze aircraft. Armed with a single 551-pound bomb, kamikaze pilots were instructed to release their bomb while in their dive, just before impacting their target ship. This created two projectiles and thus a better chance for success. (Author’s Collection)

Captured Japanese Nakajima B5N2 "Kate" aircraft arriving at Jacquinot Bay, New Britain. The B5N2 was used as a torpedo bomber, horizontal bomber, search and patrol aircraft and for anti-submarine work. When equipped with the deadly and reliable Japanese Type 91 aerial torpedo, it was one of the most successful torpedo bombers of the war. (RNZAFM)

While on an anti-submarine warfare patrol on 6 June 1944 near the Caroline Islands, this late-war B5N2 fell victim to the guns of a U.S. Navy PB4Y-1 Liberator of VB-109. The aircraft crashed into the sea shortly after this photo was taken. (USNHHC)

Kawanishi H6K "Mavis." On 23 October 1942, the B-17E "Miss Fit" (41-2433), while on an anti-submarine mission, fought a 40-minute duel with this four-engine H6K4 flying boat. On fire, streaming fuel and with a heavily damaged tailplane, the H6K finally crashed and burned. (Author's Collection)

A Kawasaki Ki-61-Ia of the 37th Advanced Flying Training Unit in Formosa in 1944. To make up for the heavy aircrew losses in 1942–1943, training was rapidly expanded and several overseas Advanced Flying Training Units such as this one were formed. (NMUSAF)

The Nakajima B6N2 Tenzan "Jill" was built to replace the B5N2 "Kate" torpedo bomber. The "Jill" slowly replaced the B5N2's in Japanese Naval Air Force service from late 1943 onward, but the lack of well-trained aircrews meant the B6N2's impact was negligible. (NARA)

A D4Y1-C having its engine run up. The D4Y1 was designed to replace the D3A1 "Val" dive-bomber. The "Judy" was the fastest carrier-borne dive-bomber of the war and one of the most versatile, serving as a light bomber, night fighter and reconnaissance aircraft. (NARA)

Tracking the U.S. carriers and their various task groups proved difficult for the Japanese. Here a Kawanishi H8K2 "Emily" snooper is shot down by F6F Hellcats off the Gilbert Islands in September 1943. The H8K2 was undoubtedly one of the finest Japanese warplanes to see operational service during the war. Possessing exceptional performance, it was the fastest flying boat to see action, and its hydrodynamic qualities were superior to British, American and German designs. (NARA)

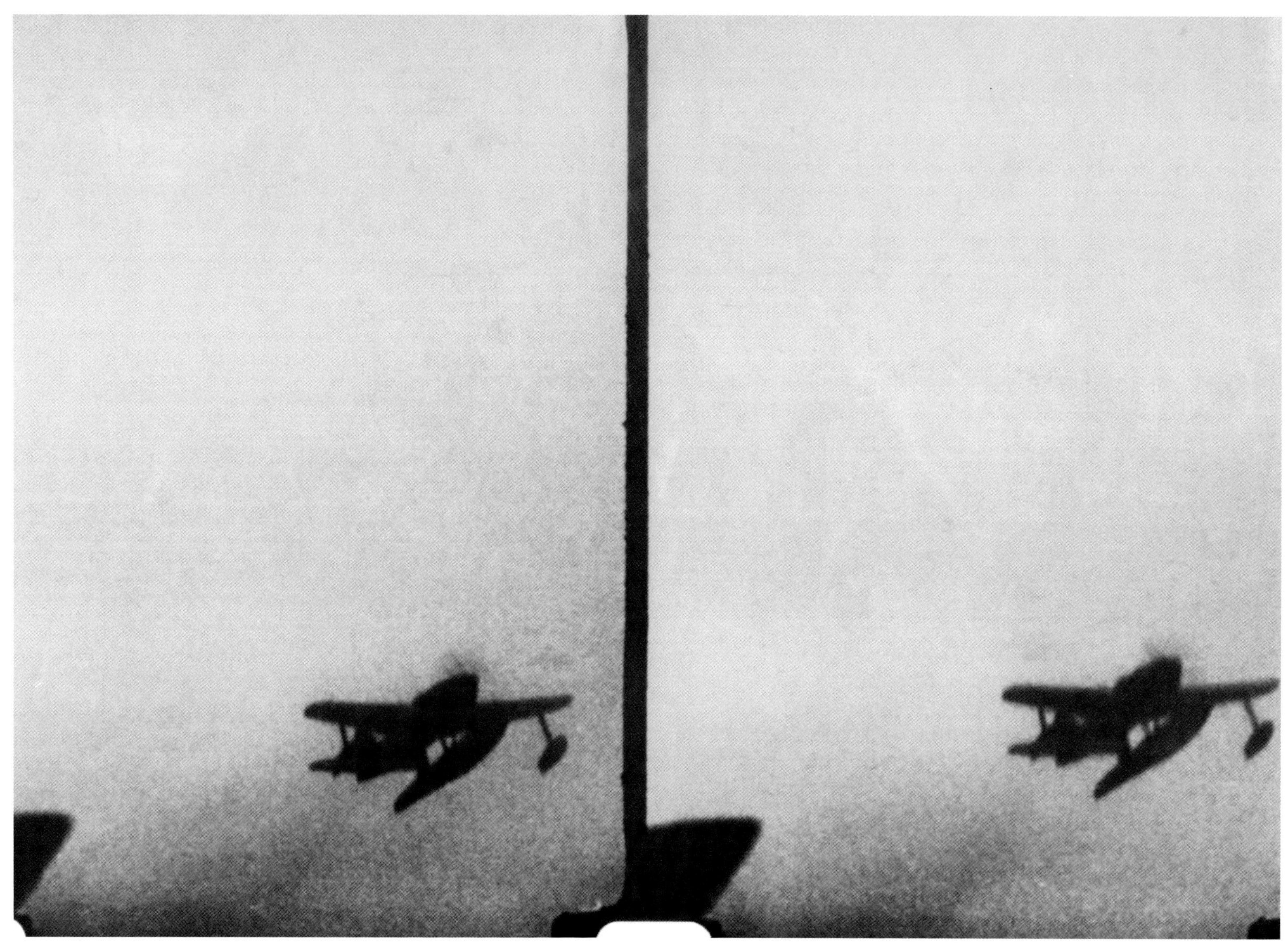

A rare gun-camera image of a Kawanishi K1K1 "Rex" floatplane-fighter shot down during U.S. carrier strikes on Kyushu on 12 March 1945. With just 97 aircraft built, the K1K1 saw limited service, but Japanese pilots were impressed with its outstanding maneuverability, thanks to its combat flaps. (NARA)

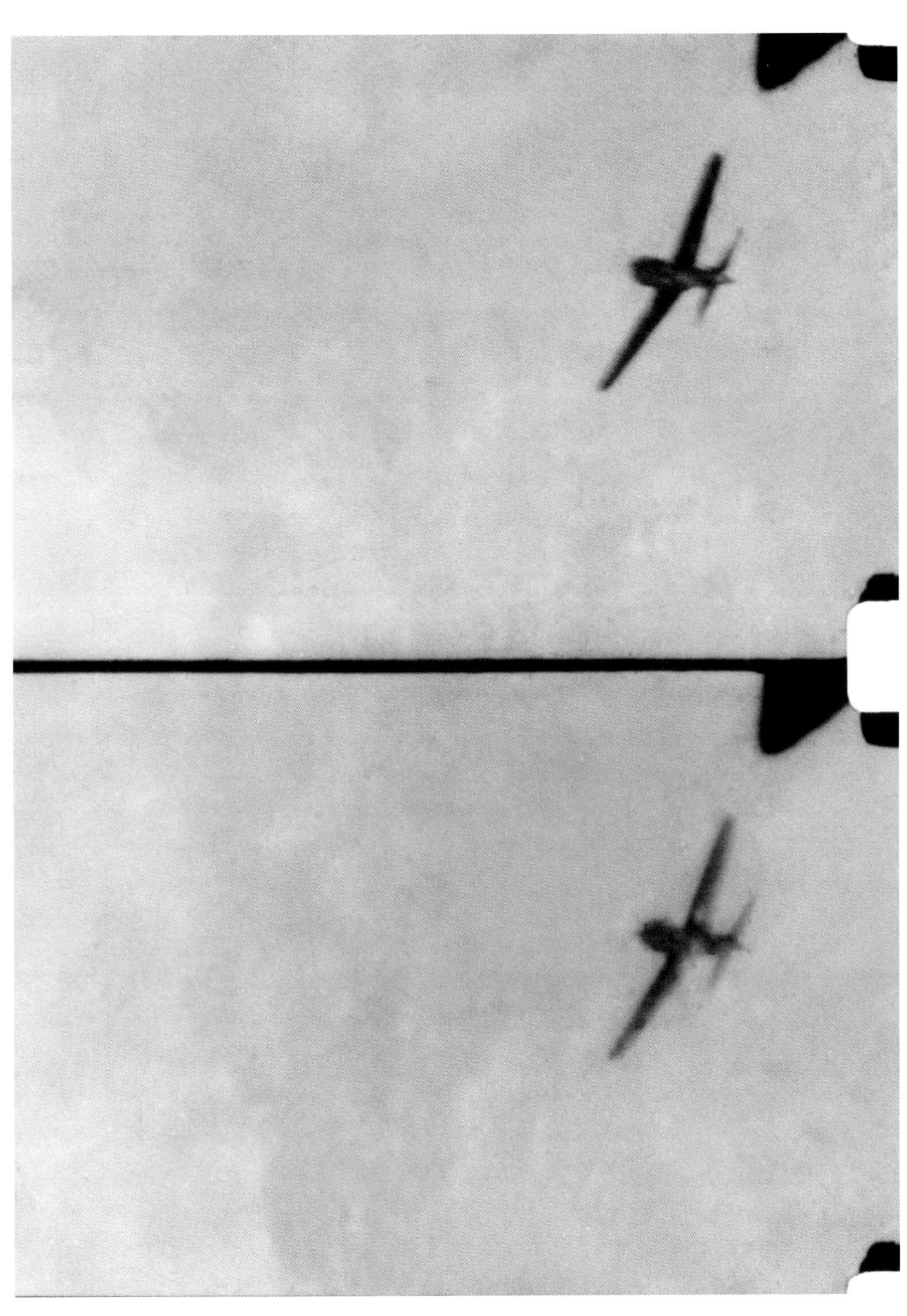

A gun-camera image of a Nakajima Ki-84 "Frank" under attack by an American Corsair from the carrier *Bunker Hill* off the coast of Japan on 12 March 1945. The Ki-84's light weight, superior maneuverability and rate of climb, coupled with its heavy armament, made it a dangerous opponent in the hands of an experienced pilot. (NARA)

A Mitsubishi G4M2 Type 1 "Betty" bomber goes down in flames after being hit by gunners from a PB2Y-3 Coronado patrol bomber in the central Pacific in 1944. The G4M had the largest production run of Japanese bombers during the war, with 2,446 being built. It would see action on every front from the first day of the Pacific war to V-J Day. (USNHHC)

A captured and damaged Nakajima Ki-43 Hayabusa "Oscar" at Lashio, Burma, on 11 March 1945. By late 1942 the Japanese Army Air Force's Ki-43 was steadily outclassed by new Allied fighters, but it soldiered on until war's end. The Ki-43 was the most widely produced Japanese army fighter of the war, and more Japanese pilots achieved ace status in this aircraft than in any other. (Author's Collection)

This reconnaissance photograph shows a Japanese Nakajima N1K1 Gekko "Irving" night fighter and what appears to be three Ki-21 "Sally" bombers at Lakunai Airdrome, Rabaul, New-Britain, in 1943. The Gekko night fighter had no forward firing armament but was fitted with twin obliquely mounted 20 mm cannons mounted dorsally and ventrally. (Author's Collection)

A Mitsubishi Ki-21 "Sally" caught on the ground at Namlea, Boeroe Island, on 3 October 1944. Low-level strafing and bombing attacks using parachute fragmentation bombs, as seen here, by 5th Air Force B-25's and A-20's proved devastating. Japanese anti-aircraft defenses and fighters were unable to stop these constant attacks. (NARA)

A trio of Nakajima Ki-44 "Tojos" of the 70th Sentai are run up by mechanics using a Toyota KC truck. The Ki-44 had a superb gun platform and possessed excellent dive-and-climb characteristics, which permitted fast hit-and-run tactics to be employed. It was a radical departure from the traditional Japanese slow-speed turning tactics. (Author's Collection)

A burning "Zeke" passes over the fantail just before crash-diving onto the flight deck of USS *Intrepid* (CV-11) on 25 November 1944. A piece of the wing as well as other debris have been shot off by the ship's anti-aircraft fire. (USNHHC)

Nakajima Ki-84-Ia "Hayates" of the 2nd Chutai, 73rd Sentai, seen here in late 1944. Introduced in May 1944, the small number of Ki-84's were often outnumbered, and when facing well-trained and well-equipped U.S Navy and U.S. Army Air Force squadrons, they suffered heavy losses. This unit would virtually cease to exist by March 1945. (NARA)

Two Kawanishi N1K2-J Shiden-Kai Model 21 fighters warm up for a ferry flight to Yokosuka after the war. Too few in numbers to have any impact in the aerial battles over Japan, the Shiden-Kai was considered by Japanese and Allied pilots to be the best fighter in the Japanese Naval Air Force. (Author's Collection)

By July 1945 both the Japanese Army Air Force and Naval Air Force had all but ceded air superiority over Japan to the Allies. These burning "Bettys" at Honshu airfield in Japan attest to the Allies' overwhelming air power presence. (NARA)

Lost in the hail of bursting anti-aircraft fire, smoke and spray from near misses, a solitary Zero-sen kamikaze skims the waves and roars toward the battleship USS *Missouri*. The battleship's twin 5-inch gun turret is pointed straight at the incoming Zero. Kamikaze attacks first began in October 1944 and lasted until the last day of the war. Approximately 3,000 suicide missions were flown, with just 367 hitting or just missing the intended target. (NARA)

The Yokosuka P1Y1 Ginga "Frances" was fast and hard to intercept, making it one of the most effective kamikaze aircraft. Fortunately for the Allies, only a small number, just over 1,000, were built. With the lack of well-trained pilots, it was never a real threat. (NARA)

The Mitsubishi Ki-67 Type 4 "Hiryu" heavy bomber entered service in late 1944 and had little or no impact on the war. While classified as a heavy bomber, it was in fact more of medium bomber with a bombload of just 2,360 pounds. In comparison, the American B-25 medium was capable of lifting 6,000 pounds of bombs. Just 698 were produced, with a small number being used as kamikaze aircraft in the late stages of the war. (NARA)

Mitsubishi J2M3 Raidens of the 1st Hikotai of the 302nd Kokutai at Atsugi Airfield in 1945. Meant to replace the Zero-sen, the J2M3 didn't enter service until December 1943 and didn't make its combat debut until the battle of the Marianas Islands in September 1944. Production was limited to just 470 aircraft. (NARA)

A lineup of A6M5c Type 52c Zero-sen's of the 252nd Kokutai in Japan in the summer of 1945. In the hands of a highly skilled pilot the Zero-sen was still a deadly opponent even at this late stage of the war. Its heavy armament of three 13.2 mm machine guns and two 20 mm cannons gave it a heavy punch. (Author's Collection)

This wrecked A6M5 Zero-sen stands in testament to the overwhelming power of the American and Royal Navy's fast carrier task forces in 1945. By July 1945 the U.S. Fast Carrier Task Force comprised 14 *Essex*-type fleet carriers and six Independence-class light carriers with 1,404 aircraft. (Author's Collection)

The debris of defeat. The Nakajima G5N2 "Liz" four-engine navy long-range attack bomber proved disappointing, with just six being built. Even if the Japanese had been able to build large numbers, they didn't have the fuel or aircrews to man these large aircraft. (NARA)

A fully loaded Ju 88A-4 being made ready for another attack on 6 October 1943. While the Finnish Air Force fought valiantly and performed well, it was in dire need of modern aircraft. Finally in April 1943, a contract to purchase 24 new Ju 88A-4's was signed with Germany. In May the new aircraft flew their first mission. (SA-Kuva)

FINLAND

Finnish Air Force

In 1937 the Finnish Air Force created a five-year development plan which called for the acquisition of more fighter aircraft. The Finns believed that any enemy attacking their country would rely heavily on bombers without fighter escort. With limited funds, and with the major European powers focused on their own rearmament programs, the Finns turned to the Netherlands and purchased 35 Fokker D.XXI fighters and then purchased 18 obsolete Bristol Bulldog fighters from the British. Fortunately for the Finns, they were able to purchase 18 Blenheim Mk I's from the British in 1936 along with a license to manufacture the aircraft.

As tension with the Soviet Union grew, the Finns took what aircraft they could get and ordered Italian Fiat G.50, American Brewster Model 239, Curtiss Hawk 75A, British Hawker Hurricane and Gloster Gladiator fighters with deliveries beginning in 1940. At the outbreak of the Winter War on 30 November 1939, the Finnish Air Force had just 145 aircraft to defend against the 900 of the Soviet Union.

Combat Aircraft Avalable November 1939
Fighters: 45
Bombers: 73

A Brewster 239 Buffalo showing its effective winter camouflage. Much maligned by the most Western air forces that flew it, the Buffalo proved a winner with the Finns. During the Continuation War with the Soviet Union in 1941, one squadron of Buffalos accounted for 24 Soviet aircraft on 9 July and another 13 on 12 August. (SA-Kuva)

FINLAND

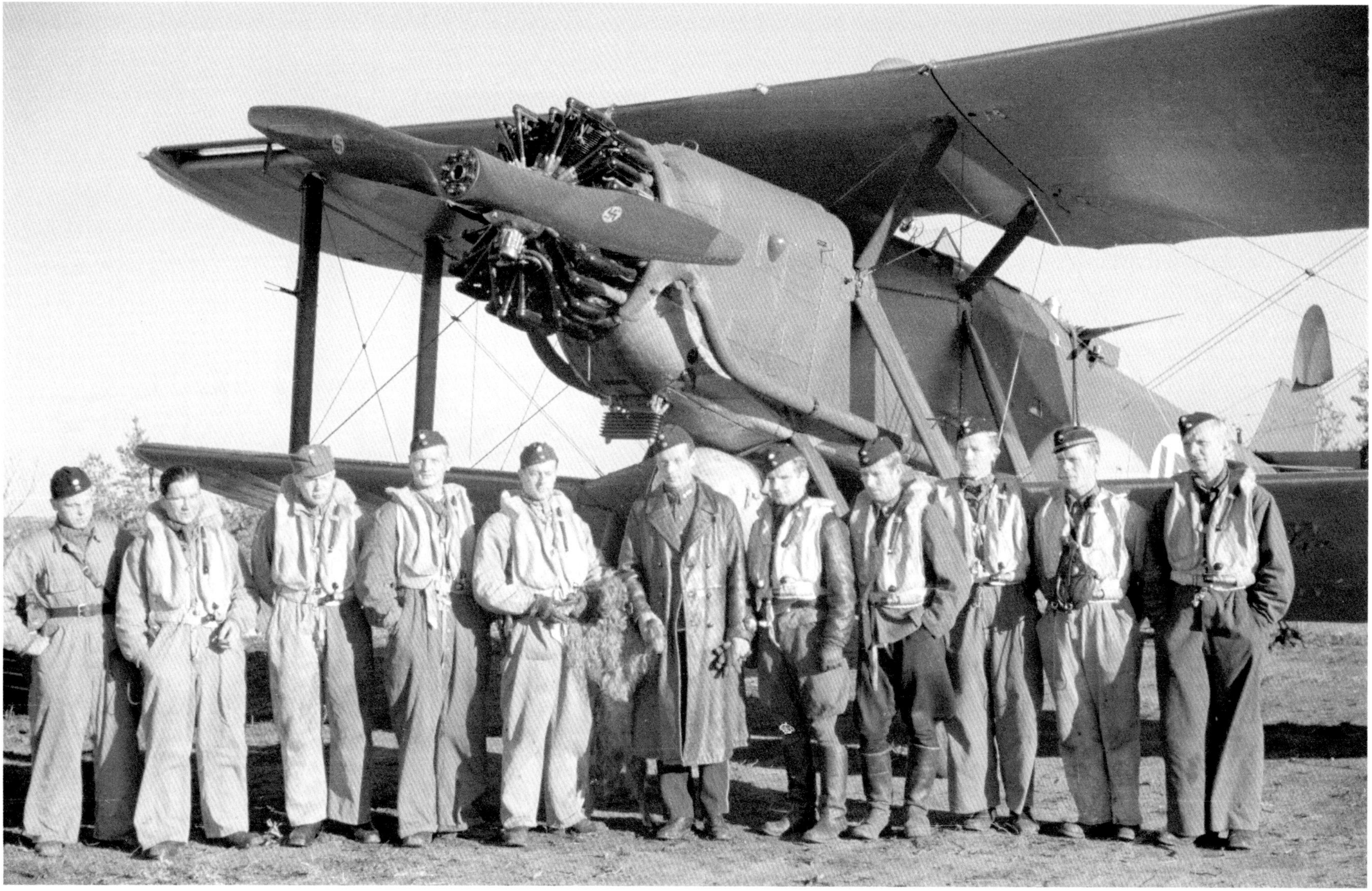

A Finnish aircrew poses in front of their Blackburn Ripon IIF. A total of 25 of these aircraft were license-built prior to the outbreak of the Winter War in November 1939. Vulnerable to daylight fighter attack, the Ripons were restricted to night bombing missions. (SA-Kuva)

In March 1943, prior to the arrival of new Ju 88's, the Finns received their first Bf 109G-2's. Here, three Bf 109G-2's of HLeLv 34 stand ready on 24 April 1943. Finland received a total of 48 Bf 109G-2's, and Germany agreed to replace any aircraft lost in combat from German stocks. (SA-Kuva)

This Gladiator II is undergoing armament maintenance. The Gladiator II was armed with four .303-caliber Browning machine guns. In January and February 1940, the Finns received 30 Gladiator II's from Great Britian. Although only a low number of fighters were available at the beginning of the Winter War in November 1939, Finnish fighter pilots were highly trained and well indoctrinated in modern fighter tactics. (SA-Kuva)

By March 1940 some 55 Gloster Gladiators, designated J-8's by the Finns, had been delivered to the Finnish Air Force. When Finland joined the Germans in Operation *Barbarossa* in June 1941, it had 14 J-8B's on strength along with a mix of British, American, French, Dutch and Italian fighters, making it the most cosmopolitan air force in the world. (SA-Kuva)

At the beginning of the Winter War, the Finnish Air Force had two squadrons of Bristol Blenheim Mk I's. During the campaign they carried out reconnaissance flights and attacked Soviet troop concentrations and airfields. (SA-Kuva)

The Fokker D.XXI was the mainstay of the Finnish Air Force when war broke out in November 1939. They had 36 aircraft available for combat. Completely outnumbered by the Soviets, Finnish pilots were given strict orders to avoid fighter duels and concentrate on shooting down bombers. With sound tactics, training and discipline, Finnish fighter pilots ended the Winter War with 207 enemy aircraft destroyed against a loss of 53 of their own aircraft. (SA-Kuva)

One of the most advanced fighters in the Finnish arsenal was the Curtiss Hawk H-75. After the fall of France, the Germans began selling aircraft captured from the French Air Force. In late 1940 the first of 29 Hawk H-75A-3's and A-6's from French and Norwegian stocks arrived in Finland. (SA-Kuva)

Between late 1940 and the end of 1942, Germany supplied 57 French MS.406 fighters to Finland. At the outbreak of the Continuation War, 21 MS.406's were ready for combat. Here, two MS.406's of 1/LeLv 28 are parked on the grass awaiting their next mission. (SA-Kuva)

A captured Savoia Marchetti SM.79 at Sidi Barrani Airfield in North Africa. The S.79 was the backbone of the Italian Air Force, and most of its bomber and torpedo bomber squadrons were equipped with it. It would also prove itself as one of the war's best land-based torpedo bombers. (Author's Collection)

ITALY

Italian Air Force

When Italy entered the war on 10 June 1940, the Germans had overrun Holland, Belgium and Luxembourg and forced the British Expeditionary Force in France to evacuate at Dunkirk. France would fall just 15 days later. These quick victories caught the Italian armed forces in the middle of their long-term rearmament program. The plan, called R for 'Rinnovamento' (Renewal), was still two years away from being complete. The combination of the Italian industry's inability to cope with a series of problems in the production of modern, stressed-skinned monoplane fighters and bombers meant the air force lagged behind its opponents. Italy's modest industrial infrastructure did not have the size or resources to match those of France, Britain and Germany.

By the mid-1930s, the Italian Air Force frontline units comprised SIAI S.81 bombers, Fiat CR.32 fighters, IMAM Ro.37 scouts and the CRDA Z.501. The majority of these were fabric covered. At the outbreak of war there were only two modern factories, Reggaine producing airframes and Alfa Romeo producing engines. Overshadowing these problems was Italy's history of aviation achievements. Having established several world aviation records during the 1920s and 1930s, Italian aviation was held in high regard around the world. From 1936 to 1939 Italian fighters and bombers fought with great success against the Republican forces during the Spanish Civil War.

Countries like Sweden, Hungary, Belgium and Finland considered the Italian designs to be superior and were eager to buy Fiat CR.42's, G.50's and Reggaine Re 2000's. Unfortunately for the Italians, this led to a false sense of superiority and satisfaction with little regard to what was happening in the rest of Europe, Japan and the United States. At the outbreak of hostilities, the total strength of the air force consisted of 3,269 aircraft, of which only 1,795 were considered combat ready. The frontline force comprised just 542 fighters — 77 Macchi C.200's, 88 Fiat G.50's, 200 Fiat CR.42's and 177 CR.32's. Both the CR.32 and CR.42 were biplane fighters.

Combat Aircraft Available June 1940
Fighters: 542
Bombers: 783
Reconnaissance: 151

ITALY

Macchi MC.200's of the 386th Squadron on a Russian airfield in May 1942. One of the great defects of Italian fighters was their weak armament. The MC.200 was armed with just two fuselage-mounted Breda-SAFAT 12.7 mm machine guns. (Author's Collection)

A Fiat CR.42 of 162nd *Squadriglia* based at Rhodes in the Aegean islands in June 1941. These fighters provided local defense and shipping escort duties. At the beginning of the war the Italian Air Force had 200 CR.42's deemed fully operational. (Author's Collection)

Fiat G.50's of the 154th Group, 395th Squadron in Albania in January 1941 during the invasion of Greece. When the Italians invaded on 28 October 1940, the Italian Air Force committed some 300-combat aircraft of which 29 were G.50 fighters. (Author's Collection)

The IMAM Ro.41 was originally designed as a light biplane fighter. Underpowered, the Ro.41 proved too slow for combat and was relegated to a training role. (Author's Collection)

The Italian Air Force employed a variety of multi-engine aircraft during the war. A pilot's ability to recognize and identify the enemy quickly often meant the difference between victory and defeat. This aircraft recognition poster was produced by the British Air Ministry. (Author's Collection)

The Fiat BR.20 featured all-metal construction but was handicapped by unreliable engines which were never up to international standards. With a limited payload and range, the BR.20, like many aircraft in the Italian Air Force, was already obsolete when Italy entered the war in June 1940. (Author's Collection)

A pilot stands beside his flak-damaged MC.200. This aircraft belonged to the 21st Group based in Ukraine in 1942. When Mussolini declared war against the Soviet Union in June 1941, he sent troops and a small air contingent of just 85 aircraft with four squadrons equipped with MC.200 fighters as support. (Author's Collection)

The Macchi MC.202 was arguably one of the best Italian fighters of the war. Powered by the license-built German DB 601 engine, it had a top speed of 370 mph and was the equal of the Spitfire Mk V. Italian industry was unable to produce the number of MC.202s needed for effective combat use, causing the Italian Air Force to soldier on with the MC.200 and CR.42. (Author's Collection)

In 1943 the Italian Air Force received 114 Bf 109G's from Luftwaffe stocks. Most of these fighters were lost in the battle for Sicily that began in July. This photograph shows a Bf 109G-6 of the 165th Squadron at Sciacca, Sicily, in April 1943. (Author's Collection)

A CANT Z.1007 bomber based in Sicily is getting ready for a bombing mission over Malta in 1941. At the beginning of the war, the Italian Air Force had 87 Z.1007's on strength with just 38 being serviceable. The CANT Z.1007 was one of the Italians' best bombers and proved itself during the long air campaign against Malta. (Author's Collection)

This photo of a Luftwaffe Bf 109G-6 and an ANR MC.205 flying in formation in early 1944 was taken to suggest that German and Italian forces were cooperating closely. This was far from the case, and after a few joint missions in the summer of 1944, cooperation between the forces was discontinued. (Author's Collection)

ITALY

Republican Air Force

The Allied invasion of Sicily in July 1943 and the continued bombing of Rome led to the dismissal of Benito Mussolini and the dissolution of the Fascist Party. On 3 September the Allied armies invaded mainland Italy, and a new government in the south was formed, eager to sign an armistice. The country was now effectively split in two, with the Italian Air Force also breaking into two factions. At the time of the armistice, the majority of what remained of the Italian Air Force was based in central and northern Italy. The German high command wished to recruit as many Italian air and ground crew into the Luftwaffe as possible. Those who didn't volunteer were given an ultimatum: join the Luftwaffe or face deportation to labor camps in Germany. At the same time, the Luftwaffe commandeered over 1,000 aircraft in central and northern Italy. By October 1943 the Republican Air Force reached an agreement with the Luftwaffe which allowed the Italians to form their own independent squadrons of fighters, bombers, and torpedo bombers. The Republican Air Force also urged former aircrews to join in the defense of the homeland against the continued Allied bombing.

By January 1944, 6,997 men had answered the call and enlisted in the Republican Air force. At the same time, the Germans promised to return the confiscated aircraft and Italian personnel who had been taken into Luftwaffe service. With the main Italian aircraft and engine factories located in the northern part of the country, the Republican Air Force could reequip several squadrons with the latest Italian aircraft which included the superb Macchi MC.205V Serie III and Fiat G.55/I fighters. But as Allied bombing increased, supplies of these aircraft dwindled, forcing the Germans to reequip their Italian allies with a large number of Bf 109G-6, G-10, G-14 and K-4 fighters.

A well-camouflaged Bf 109G-10/AS of the 1st Group ANR warms up for one of its final operations in March 1945. On 19 April, the 1st Group flew its last mission of the war, claiming one B-24 Liberator shot down. (Author's Collection)

A Reggaine Re 2005 of the ANR is seen here in 1944. Just 48 of these superb fighters were built. At the time of the armistice with the Allies, 13 were seized by the Germans and eventually served with the Republican Air Force in the north. Powered by a license-built DB 605A-1 engine, the Re 2005 had a top speed of 390 mph at 22,800 feet and was heavily armed with three 20 mm MG 151 cannons and two 12.7 mm Breda-SAFAT machine guns. (Author's Collection)

A Fiat G.55 Serie I of the 2nd Group Republican Air Force in July 1944. The G.55 was the best Italian fighter of the war. Equal to and sometimes better than the Bf 109G, Fw 190A and Spitfire Mk IX. Maximum speed was 385 mph at 22,965 feet. With just over 100 aircraft built, the G.55 saw limited service with the Republican Air Force. By the spring of 1945 none remained in service. (Author's Collection)

Two Republican Air Force SM.79bis torpedo bombers showing the new black camouflage scheme for night operations. On 5 January 1945, two SM.79's sank a 5,000-ton ship in the Adriatic; it was the last Republican Air Force torpedo attack of the war. (Author's Collection)

In July 1940, when the Vichy Air Force was formed, it comprised a motley collection of modern, mediocre and clearly obsolete aircraft. One of those obsolete aircraft was the LeO H-257bis. A total of 53 found their way to the Vichy forces and served in a secondary role as transport, target towing and training aircraft. (Author's Collection)

FRANCE

French Air Force

After the fall of France at the end of June 1940, the French Air Force was stronger, both quantitatively and qualitatively, than in September 1939. In July 1940 the seven best fighter groups retreated to North Africa, and three more fighter groups went to Syria equipped with a mix of Curtiss H-75, D.520 and MS.406 fighters. Bomber groups included modern types like the American-built Martin 167, Douglas DB-7's and French Lioré-et-Olivier LeO 45 medium bombers.

Article 4 of the armistice agreement between Germany and France covered the demobilization and disarmament of the French armed forces. This quickly changed with the British attack on the French Fleet at Mers el Kebir near Oran on 3 July 1940. Following the raid, the Germans agreed to the creation of the Vichy French Air Force under control of the newly established Vichy government. To defend against further British aggression, Germany granted the Vichy government an air force strength of 1,040 aircraft stationed in France, its colonies and its mandate regions around the globe.

Initially, the Germans put a number of constraints on the Vichy French Air Force to reduce its effectiveness. Pilots were not allowed to fly more than two training hours a week and had to remain within 9.3 miles of their airfields. By March 1941, after much lobbying by French authorities, Germany granted concessions and allowed the number of aircraft to increase to 1,071.

Combat Aircraft Available July 1940

Fighters: 435

Bombers: 292

Reconnaissance: 275

Torpedo Bombers: 38

FRANCE

A new Bloch MB 174 awaits deployment to North Africa. The MB 174 was a reconnaissance light bomber capable of carrying eight 110-pound bombs internally. The MB 174 was a versatile aircraft, and at the time of the armistice only one squadron was able to keep its MB 174's in Tunisia. The aircraft would see action against Allied forces during Operation *Torch* in November 1940. (Author's Collection)

A lineup of Vichy French Navy Latecoere Late 298 seaplanes based in Karouba Algeria, July 1940. The Late 298 was a torpedo/maritime reconnaissance bomber capable of lifting a 1,499-pound torpedo. At the time of the German invasion of France, six squadrons with approximately 81 aircraft were available. After the armistice of June 1940, the Vichy Air Force was allowed to retain some units based in Algeria. (Author's Collection)

A Dewoitine D.520 GC III/6 in France in 1941. As France's best fighter, the D.520 would see combat against Royal Air Force Hurricanes and Gladiators; SAAF P-40's over French-controlled Syria in June 1941; and U.S. Navy F4F Wildcats, RN Seafires and Sea Hurricanes and U.S. Army Air Force P-40's during Operation *Torch*, the Allied invasion of North Africa in November 1942. At the time of the invasion of North Africa, the Vichy French had 38 D.520's and 40 H-75's on strength. (Author's Collection)

Three Curtiss-Hawk H-75A's of GC I/4 over Dakar, Senegal, in 1942. At the time of the armistice, all the Fighter Groups equipped with Curtiss H-75's took refuge in North Africa. There were approximately 186 aircraft in North Africa, with 45 aircraft remaining in France. (Author's Collection)

The MS.406 was the least capable fighter deployed by the Vichy French, but at the beginning of the war it was the most numerous fighter aircraft in their air force. During the battle for Syria-Lebanon in 1941, MS.406 and D.520 fighters were credited with 34 aerial victories. The British and Australians lost 27 aircraft. Vichy forces lost 128 aircraft to all causes during the campaign. (Author's Collection)

The Glenn Martin 167 was the most capable bomber in Vichy service. While relatively fast, it had a small bombload. The 167 would see action during the Syria-Lebanon campaign against the British in 1941 and again during Operation *Torch* in November 1942. (Author's Collection)

The Italian Reggaine Re 2000 was Hungary's most modern fighter at the beginning of World War II. They ordered 70 from Italy and built a further 200 under license between 1940 and 1942. Its armament was weak, with just two 12.7 mm Breda-SAFAT machine guns. (Author's Collection)

HUNGARY

Royal Hungarian Air Force

Out of the ashes of World War I, the once mighty Hungarian Kingdom was reduced to just a small country. The Treaty of Trianon of June 1920 reduced Hungary's army to just 35,000 men, and military aviation and the manufacture of military aircraft was forbidden. Working in secret, the Hungarians began to build a small air force starting in 1928. Shortly after, Italy was asked to supply 400 aircraft and offered Fiat CR.20 biplane fighters and Caproni Ca. 101 parasol monoplanes. This acquisition was followed by an order for 76 Fiat CR.32 fighters in 1935–36. These deliveries were augmented by a number of German aircraft, including 66 Junkers Ju 86K-2 bombers, Heinkel 46E-2s close-support aircraft, 5 He 45's and 18 Heinkel He 70 light bombers. On 1 January 1939, the Royal Hungarian Air Force became an independent branch of the military.

In 1939 the Hungarian air force comprised 252 aircraft and 6,075 men but was still 52 aircraft below its desired strength. Promise of German aircraft faltered because Berlin feared Hungary would use its air force against Romania, German's ally. To fill the breach, Italy once again offered to supply more aircraft. A total of 42 Fiat CR.42's were delivered, and in 1939 an order for 70 Reggaine Re 2000 Falco I monoplane fighters was placed. This was followed by an order for 71 Caproni Ca 135bis twin-engine bombers that were delivered in the summer of 1940. By May 1941 the Royal Hungarian Air Force had 390 combat aircraft in its inventory.

Combat Aircraft Available May 1941

Fighters: 174

Bombers: 71

Reconnaissance: 136

HUNGARY

A Hungarian CR.42 under repairs. On the day of the German attack on the Soviet Union, 22 June 1941, the Hungarian Air Force possessed 320 combat aircraft, 68 of which were Fiat CR.42 fighters. (Author's Collection)

A Junkers Ju 86K-2 bomber and six Heinkel He 70's. Used as a fast reconnaissance aircraft, the He 70 was powered by a Gnome-Rhone radial engine, giving it top speed of 224 mph. The Ju 86 was obsolete when the war began. When Hungary joined the assault against the Soviet Union, approximately 36 Ju 86's were committed to the fight. (Author's Collection)

A Fiat CR.42 on the ground after a landing mishap. The Romanians relied heavily on their fleet of obsolete CR.42 and CR.32 fighters. On the day of the German attack on the Soviet Union, the Royal Hungarian Air Force had 69 CR.42's in their inventory. (Author's Collection)

A Bf 109F-4 being prepared for flight. After months of heavy fighting and attrition on the Russian front, the Hungarians had lost close to 50 percent of their aircraft. Domestic production could not keep pace with demand, so, in March 1943, the reluctant Germans agreed to deliver 66 Bf 109F, G-2 and G-6 fighters between June 1942 and March 1944. (Author's Collection)

This Re 2000 fighter is preparing to take off. The Hungarian aviation industry did not reach its peak production until 1944; as a result, just 170 Re 2000's were built between 1943 and 1944. By this time, however, the aircraft was no longer suitable for combat and was relegated to being used as a trainer. (Author's Collection)

A Bf 109G-2 undergoing maintenance. The G-2 was powered by the DB 605A engine. Armament consisted of one 20 mm MG 151 cannon and two 7.92 mm MG 17 machine guns. Hungary was one of the few countries to license-build the Bf 109, with 92 G-4's and G-6's constructed in 1943. (Author's Collection)

A lineup of IAR 80's. With Romania's first flight in April 1939, the IAR 80 surprised many aviation experts with its top speed of 317 mph, service ceiling of 37,000 feet and rate of climb of 16,400 feet in six minutes. Total production was 400 aircraft. (Author's Collection)

ROMANIA

Royal Romanian Air Force

In March 1940 the Romanian government embarked on an ambitious plan calling for the expansion of the Royal Romanian Air Force to 84 squadrons. But the Romanian aircraft industry at the time was not large enough to equip the air force with modern aircraft. Poland was the first large-scale supplier of aircraft to Romania, delivering 50 PZL P.11 in 1934 and five PZL P.24 fighters in 1939. Another 25 P.24's were also built under license. After the fall of Poland, 200 Polish aircraft were sent to Romania.

Great Britain was late in supporting Romania. To check German influence in the Balkans, Britain, starting in 1939, supplied Romania with 40 Bristol Blenheim bombers and 12 Hawker Hurricane fighters. As a countermove, Germany supplied 30 Heinkel He 112 fighters. Italy also delivered 24 twin-engine SM.79B bombers to the Romanian air force. France's contribution was 20 Potez 63 B2 twin-engine light bombers. Since war made further deliveries of French and British aircraft impossible, Germany filled the gap with 32 He 111H-3 bombers and 50 Bf 109E-3/4 fighters.

One of the forgotten fighters of World War II was Romania's IAR 80, its most famous fighter. It's first flight in April 1939 revealed a fighter capable of reaching 317 mph. In December 1939 the government ordered 100 with another 261 ordered between August 1940 and May 1942.

Combat Aircraft Available June 1941
Fighters: 172
Bombers: 116

A Bf 109E-7 of Grupul 5. Note the three small white victory bars on the vertical tail fin. Between 22 June and 16 October 1941, the Romanian's fighter arm and anti-aircraft defenses claimed 266 Soviet aircraft shot down during those initial months of Operation *Barbarossa*. Overstating the number of aircraft shot down on both sides was rampant during the war, so the actual number was much lower. (Author's Collection)

ROMANIA

A Heinkel He 111H-3 in Romanian colors. As the war in the west progressed, deliveries of French, British and Polish aircraft dried up for Romania. Germany sold them 32 He 111H-3's. The Romanians, however, were not happy when they found that they had paid full price for aircraft that turned out to be used and not new. (Author's Collection)

A Romanian ground crew poses by their Heinkel He 112B fighter. As Romania rearmed, they bought aircraft from Poland, Great Britain and Germany. German pre-war deliveries included 30 Heinkel He 112B fighters. The He 112B's would equip two squadrons, and Romania was the only country to use the He 112B in combat. Powered by a 680-horsepower Jumo 210 engine, the He 112B had a maximum speed of 317 mph at 13,120 feet. (Author's Collection)

A pair of Bf 109E-3's in flight. On 22 June 1941, the Romanian Air Force committed 88 Bf 109E-3's to Operation *Barbarossa*, the invasion of the Soviet Union. A total of 225 fighters and fighter bombers were committed, representing about 40 percent of the Romanian Air Force's total strength. (Author's Collection)

A Romanian pilot poses in his IAR 81C. The IAR 81 was one of the first fighters in Europe to employ a bubble canopy, long before the Malcolm hood appeared on the U.S. Army Air Force P-51B/C in 1944. (Author's Collection)

A Do 17P taxing out for another mission. In 1942 Germany delivered 12 Do 17P's to Bulgaria, followed by six more in 1941. Bulgaria did not participate in the German attack on the Soviet Union, but it did assist the Luftwaffe during the Greek and Crete campaigns with Do 17's providing convoy escort and submarine patrol. (Author's Collection)

BULGARIA

Royal Bulgarian Air Force

Like Hungary, Bulgaria lost its entire air force at the end of World War I and was forbidden to have or build any military aircraft for a period of 20 years. Beginning in 1923, secret rearmament work began on a modest scale. A few months later the DAR works was established to resume aircraft and engine production. In mid-1930, Bulgaria started a rearmament policy in open defiance of the treaties signed after World War I.

But Bulgaria's weak indigenous aircraft industry forced it to seek combat aircraft elsewhere. In 1937 Bulgaria ordered 14 Polish PZL P.24B fighters and 12 PZL P.23 tactical bombers. Prior to that, Germany had delivered 12 Heinkel He 45's and 12 He 51 fighters in 1936. The following year Goering presented Bulgaria with 12 Arado Ar 65 fighters and 12 Dornier Do 11D bombers, both obsolete.

After the German occupation of Czechoslovakia in 1939, Bulgaria received a huge boost when Germany sold the disbanded Czech Air Force to Bulgaria at a huge discount. Bulgaria received 78 Avia B-534 fighters, 60 Letov S-328 reconnaissance aircraft, 32 Avia B-71 (license-built Tupolev SB bombers) and 12 Aero MB 200 bombers. The next year Germany delivered 10 Bf 109E-3 fighters and 12 Dornier Do 17P bombers. In 1940 the Bulgarian Air Force possessed 580 aircraft. An impressive number on paper, but qualitatively the air force remained second rate in action.

Combat Aircraft Available June 1940

Fighters: 102
Bombers: 62
Close Support: 34
Reconnaissance: 92

BULGARIA

A Heinkel He 51 biplane fighter. A total of 12 He 51's were delivered in 1936, and by 1939 they were clearly obsolete and relegated to a training role. (Author's Collection)

A lineup of Bulgarian Air Force Avia B-534 fighters in 1941. After the German occupation of Czechoslovakia, the Bulgarians received 78 ex-Czech air force B-534's, but a good number of these saw little service as a frontline fighter. With a top speed of just 245 mph at 14,435 feet, it was obsolete when compared to current modern monoplane fighters. (Author's Collection)

A lineup of Bf 109G-6's. Beginning in late 1943, Allied bombers began invading Bulgarian airspace, which raised alarms in Berlin. The Avia B-534 could do little against the B-24's of the U.S. Army Air Force. As a result, the Germans dispatched 16 Bf 109G-2's in late 1943 followed by 40 more G-6's in 1944. (Author's Collection)

The Letov S-328 was a Czechoslovakian designed and built two-seat reconnaissance/bomber. Capable of lifting 1,102 pounds of bombs, it has a top speed of 170 mph. Bulgaria purchased 62 aircraft from German stocks in 1939. (Author's collection)

A Slovak Bf 109E-4/B on a snow-covered runway. The canvas shroud was to keep the engine from freezing in the cold weather and make it easier to start. Slovak Bf 109 pilots achieved their first aerial victories in November 1943, when three Soviet I-153 fighters were shot down. (Author's Collection)

SLOVAKIA

Slovak Air Force

When Slovakia proclaimed its independence on 14 March 1939, it quickly singed a Protection Agreement with Germany. The young Slovak Air Force mustered a total of 300 aircraft, most of which were hopelessly outdated. The majority of the force was composed of 71 Czech-built Avia B-534 fighters and 73 Lotev S-328 biplane reconnaissance bombers. Slovakia was the only country to join Hitler's invasion of Poland, sending 35,000 troops, 20 Avia B-534's and 10 Letov S-328's to fight with the German armies. On 1 May 1941, the 11th, 12th and 13th Fighter Squadrons reorganized as the 2nd Fighter Group and the three observation squadrons as the 1st Observation Group. Just seven weeks later, these units joined Hitler's invasion of the Soviet Union.

Combat Aircraft Available May 1941
Fighters: 71
Bombers: 3
Reconaissance: 87

Three Bf 109's of the Slovak Air Force flying on a training mission. By late October 1941, it was clear the B-534 was no match for Soviet fighters. In response, the Germans re-equipped one Slovak squadron with Bf 109E-4/B's. A total of 27 Bf 109E variants would be delivered to the Slovak Air Force by 1942. (Author's Collection)

A Slovak Air Force Avia-B-534 in Ukraine in 1941. The Czech-built B-534 provided the backbone of the fledgling Slovak Air Force's 60 aircraft. First flown on 25 May 1933, the B-534 was a robust biplane with a fixed armament of four 7.92 mm machine guns and a top speed of 236 mph. By 1939 it was hopelessly outdated. (Author's Collection)

A captured Croatian Air Force Bf 109G-10/AS. German-supplied Bf 109G-10 and G-14 fighters did not reach the Croatian Air Force until January 1945, but by that time the military situation had taken a dramatic turn for the worst, and the small number of Bf 109's available had no impact on the outcome of the war. (Author's Collection)

CROATIA

Croatian Air Force

On 10 April 1941, the Croatian Air Force, one of the last European forces to come into existence during World War II, was formed. It was just nine days after the proclamation of the independent Croatian state. Made up largely of former members of the Yugoslavian Air Force, the newly minted Croatian Air Force's first task was to acquire and salvage the aircraft and equipment that had survived the fighting between German and Yugoslavian forces and had not been confiscated by the Germans or Italians.

After the German attack on the Soviet Union in June 1941, Croatian Chief of State Ante Pavelic wrote to Adolf Hitler and offered Croatian air and army assets to fight on the eastern front. In July 1941 the Germans opened an initial flight training school at Zagreb. Shortly after, the 10th and 11th Fighter squadrons with Bf 109E's and the 12th and 13th Bomber squadrons with Do 17Z's formed the Croatian-Luftwaffen Legion, with 300 Croatian airmen going to Germany for training.

Combat Aircraft Available June 1941
Fighters: 22
Bombers: 22

The Croatian Air Force received just nine Fiat G.50's and one two-seat version in 1942. By mid-1944 the Allies had achieved almost complete air supremacy over southern Eastern Europe. Flying and fighting in the slower Fiat G.50, capable of 293 mph at 16,400 feet, against the more advanced Allied aircraft became an exercise in futility. (Author's Collection)

Photo Credits

All photographs courtesy of the Author's Collection
except as noted:

AAM – Aviodrome Aviation Museum, Netherlands
Andrew Thomas
CVA – City of Vancouver Archives
CWM – Canadian War Museum – CWM 19850452-082
Daniel Brackx
Frank Mitchell
LC – Library of Congress
Little Friends – littlefriends.co.uk
Matthew Willis
NARA – U. S. National Archives and Records Administration
NASM – Smithsonian National Air and Space Museum
NIMH – Nederlands Instituut voor Militaire Historie
NMUSAF – National Museum of the United States Air Force
RNZAFM – Air Force Museum of New Zealand
SA-Kuva – Finnish Wartime Photographic Archive
USNHHC – U.S. Naval History and Heritage Command

Index